THE KILLING OF WILLIAM RUFUS
An Investigation in the New Forest

BY THE SAME AUTHOR

POLITICAL HISTORY
The Map of Europe (1934-1936)

NAVAL HISTORY
The Silent Victory

BIOGRAPHY

Baden-Powell at Mafeking
The Triumph of Integrity: a portrait of General de Gaulle
Mad, is he? The character and achievements of General Wolfe

FIRST WORLD WAR ADVENTURE
An Escaper's Log
Wind in the Wires
Escapers All (in collaboration)

FICTION
Fortune of War
Ashby's Downfall
Brierley

The scene of the killing: the Rufus Stone at a range of 17 yards.

THE KILLING OF WILLIAM RUFUS

An Investigation in the New Forest

Duncan Grinnell-Milne

DAVID & CHARLES: NEWTON ABBOT

7153 4247 9

© *Duncan Grinnell-Milne*
1968

Printed in Great Britain by
Clarke, Doble & Brendon Ltd Plymouth
for David & Charles (Publishers) Limited
Newton Abbot Devon

CONTENTS

LIST OF ILLUSTRATIONS

The author wishes to acknowledge with gratitude the help and advice given him by the Deputy Surveyor of the New Forest and by members of the Forestry Commission at The Queen's House, Lyndhurst, Hampshire.

INTRODUCTORY NOTE

THIS is a work of medieval history. It is also a detective story. The two things, being more or less synonymous, usually mix well enough. Here, however, the blending has not been so easy because, whilst the history is securely based upon documentary evidence, the work of detection has had to rely very largely upon my own searching examination of a small wood in the New Forest. To make sure that the results of the examination are clearly understood it has seemed essential to give the reasons not only for every deduction made, but also, and almost literally, for every step taken. This has involved me in a personal narrative since, although it may be agreed that sufficient evidence has been adduced to justify the opinions expressed and the theories advanced, there are no other historians to tell the story for me; not, at least, the story of what happened in the Stricknage Wood. I can only hope that I shall be forgiven this unprofessional intrusion of the first personal singular.

D. G-M.
1968

I

START OF THE QUEST

THE day came when I could wait no longer. The urge to look into an unsolved historical mystery gave me no peace. Who killed William II, king of the English, in the New Forest on Thursday, August 2nd, 1100? Who, how, and why? Was it murder or accidental death? A cunning plot or the merest chance? So many questions, to which so many scholars have found no certain answers.

One morning towards the end of July, 1963, I decided to tackle the problem at once, and to start with an investigation upon the spot. Aware that working alone I should have to double the roles of Holmes and Watson, I took with me a folder containing all the home-work already done on the case and equipped myself in addition with notebook, map and compass. Then, after sending a wire asking a friend to meet me at Southampton, I set out by train from Waterloo.

Hardly had the journey started than the reaction set in. Why in the name of commonsense, I asked myself, was I going to delve into this ancient mystery 'on the spot'? What did I expect to find: Norman footprints in the dust? All very well to argue that, since a significant part of my boyhood had been spent in the Forest, at least I knew the lie of the land; if I knew it so well, why bother to go there? Because, for one thing, very few professional historians have ever done so; and, for another, because the right place to start a criminal investigation must surely be at the scene of the crime, provided of course one is sure of the scene. But just then I was not even sure that there had been a crime.

Confidence began to return when, with the train running at speed through Winchester, I looked back through the trees to

11

glimpse the great bulk of the cathedral, its massive square tower no less impressive for the fleeting view. More than one clue to the mystery has long lain buried there; the silent Rufus, once so boisterous and formidable, lies there yet, despite the jostling his bones received when the central tower fell down upon them in the year after his death. Naturally, at the tower's collapse, many a medieval cleric exclaimed that it must be a sign of divine displeasure at the presence in the church of one who had scoffed at the Church. All the more commendable that the monkish chronicler William of Malmesbury should deride superstition and make so factual a report: 'it would have collapsed in any case, even had he not been buried there, because it was badly built.'— honest reporting that gives confidence in his reliability when he tells the story of the King's death.

And this is how he tells it in his *Gesta Regum* :[1]

After dinner, in the evening of the second of August in the year Eleven Hundred, the King rode into the Forest with a few companions to hunt deer. The party split up in the woods, and the King was left alone with Walter Tirel.

The sun was setting when a stag passed near by; and the King, drawing his bow, loosed an arrow which hit the mark but failed to kill. Slightly wounded, the animal ran off to the west whilst the King watched intently for some time, raising a hand to shield his eyes against the rays of the sun.

Just then another stag passed by. Tirel shot at it and missed; but the arrow flew on and, by mischance, struck the King beyond. Clutching at the shaft where it protruded from his breast the King fell forward, breaking the arrow in his body as he hit the ground and dying instantly without having uttered a word.

A dramatic story in which the scene is well set : sundown in the quiet Forest, deer running, an arrow in flight—and sudden death, without a word spoken. There is a vivid precision about it that can only have come from an eye-witness speaking immediately after the event, though it was to be some twenty-five years before

[1] See also the concise rendering given by Professor Christopher Brooke in *The Saxon and Norman Kings* and the more literal translation in Dr Margaret Murray's *God of the Witches*.

the account was published by William of Malmesbury. 'Mischance,' said the eye-witness. A few years later the view was given support, and the account to some extent amplified, by Orderic Vitalis—generally regarded as a French historian, though born in England in 1075—and the story was further developed by the Norman poet-historian Geoffrey Gaimar. So that from three contemporary chroniclers one might perhaps conclude that the King's death was due to a rather extraordinary hunting accident, were it not for the even more extraordinary circumstances that succeeded it. There was the precipitate action taken by the remaining members of the hunting party. There was Tirel's subsequent denial of any share in the accident. There was the curious unanimity of the ecclesiastical authorities in claiming, with remarkable hindsight, that the death had been widely foretold in grotesque dreams and fantastic visions. And then silence, the absence of any inquiry.

At Southampton the train was late in arriving; the friend whom I expected to meet me was later still; it was cold and beginning to rain. And when at length we were bowling along the traffic-laden highway to the west, past Redbridge and over the tidal marshes at the mouth of the Test that once formed the eastern boundary of the New Forest, the road ahead looked bleak and the farther we went the more sadly changed. From Totton to Ashurst the 'improvements' since my last visit, some years previously, were everywhere manifest. New houses, new filling-stations, new stretches of road with more coaches, buses and lorries, all seemed to declare that here was a semi-suburbanized region no longer greatly different from any other once wooded area in southern England.

Then suddenly, as we crossed the railway at Lyndhurst Road, there it was: the silent, immemorial Forest. A startling impression. Changes of detail there had been of course, but the extraordinary lack of change overall was astonishing. The tree-dotted 'lawns' were still hemmed in by thick, leafy clumps whose sides were pierced by narrow glades winding into dark recesses. The old inclosures[1] were still crossed by grass-grown rides bordered by woods so dense that even in broad daylight the shadows were black as night. Upon the fringe of thickets the oaks stood dominant, their trunks like castle walls, testifying by their great girth to the passing of uncounted centuries. And beyond the belt of woods the moors rolled to the skyline, the vast wastelands spread with heather and bracken and patches of gorse, the plains white with cotton-grass, the long ridges of red gravel, and the low-lying swamps deep and dangerous in winter.

It lies there yet, the little changed Forest of pre-history, living on almost miraculously despite the encroachments and depredations of progress. Much of it is, in fact, still the same in general aspect, and even in local detail, as when the Conqueror claimed it for his own, belatedly adding to the huge forest lands already held by the Crown this his *new* Forest. 'New' in that sense alone, for the imposition of Norman forest-law had but reaffirmed, with sharper penalties, the Danish law imposed by Cnut upon the forest that had been there since pre-history. The *Ytene* of the West Saxons—pronounced *'Itany'* like Britanny? No matter, the meaning is known: a 'furzy waste'. And the implication is clear from the word's ancient origin. This is and always was a wilderness, a forest in the true sense, not only of big timber but also of open heath and scanty pasture, of hollow bogs and arid highlands. A land that could never under any circumstances, least of all those of primitive agriculture, have supported the population claimed for it by those chroniclers who denounced, long after the event, the fearful devastation wrought by the Conqueror for his selfish pleasure.

It is hard to understand how anyone can still manage to swallow whole that ancient piece of political propaganda which Cobbett, in his *Rural Rides*, was the first to expose and which Wise so expertly contradicted in the mid-19th century. 'Many populous towns and villages and thirty-six parish churches destroyed and consumed by fire', so runs a medieval account frequently quoted

[1] All fenced areas in the New Forest are termed 'inclosures' and are so marked on all maps.

(from Walter Mapes, mid-12th century), to which Orderic Vitalis added 'sixty parishes' laid waste. Funny way to improve a game preserve; what were the deer to browse on—rubble and burnt sticks? Such a holocaust would have scared them away for years. Odd too that the contemporary Anglo-Saxon chronicler, who knew the Conqueror personally and never spared him when it came to listing his evil actions—or those of his son, Rufus, for that matter—does not once refer to any supposed devastation in the area of the New Forest. But in sober reality one may search the scanty records from long before the afforestation decree of 1079 to the Domesday survey of 1086 and never find so much as a whisper concerning those legendary population centres, let alone the name of any one of the 'sixty parishes'. And were skilled searchers to dig up the whole of the nearly two hundred square miles of what once lay under forest law they would not uncover a single stone of the 'thirty-six' legendary churches.

The truth is that they never existed, those 'many towns and villages', for the good reason that the people to fill them did not exist. The soil proves that, because—and on this all experts are agreed—the soil of the New Forest as a whole is and always has been as unproductive as any in all the south of England: 'a poor acid soil deficient in phosphates' according to a recent Forestry Commission report.[1] No doubt the sparse inhabitants of the *Ytene* —between one and two thousand at the very most—suffered hardship and injury through the drastic tightening up by the Normans of laws already existing under the Confessor and under Cnut; but it was lack of sustenance that kept their numbers down. Even today, with scientific methods and chemical fertilizers, little of the land is worth the ploughing and, where it is ploughed, the crops are light. Modern prosperity in the area is due to cattle raising and to the timber yielded by careful forestry.

Of course, where the woods grow there is good top-soil, but it is very seldom more than eighteen inches deep and in most places the trees have to spread wide their roots to find it. That they

---

[1] See also Brian Vesey-Fitzgerald on the poverty of the soil.

grow so well is largely due to the shelter provided by the Wiltshire Downs to the north, by the Isle of Wight to the south; shelter that imparts to the region a climate of relative warmth, whilst the moisture coming in from the sea on the prevailing south-westerly wind is retained almost to excess by the underlying clay. But the strictly limited areas of these shallow patches of loam mean this: that, except where artificially assisted, the woods remain static in contour, confined within natural boundaries. Any tendency to expand is halted by the surrounding areas of gravel and sand, devoid of top-soil, upon which trees cannot grow and never can have grown.

I stress this point here because my initial hopes of solving some part of the Rufus mystery 'on the spot' were based upon this quality of changelessness, an immobility enforced across the centuries by the poverty of the soil. About the lack of change there can be no doubt; all the leading writers on Forest history have noted it. One of the most recent, H. L. Edlin of the Forestry Commission, has this to say: 'Oaks and beeches that number their years by centuries stand beside heaths that the plough has never broken . . . a primeval England. There are glades, moors, and marshes, deep within the Forest, that have scarcely changed since William the Conqueror.'

At Lyndhurst, my base for the duration of the inquiry, we made a brief halt; and then drove out again, along the Romsey road. Here, probably owing to the cheerless weather, there was less traffic than usual and when we turned left and began winding between the hedgerows up the hill to Minstead the lanes were deserted. Few animals were to be seen in the fields, in the village hardly a soul, and the dense woods screening Castle Malwood were dark and silent.

None of which prepared me for the shock of dismay felt as, breasting the rise, we swung left upon the ancient and well-remembered highway flowing west over the moors, by Stoney Cross and Bratley and Picket Post, to distant Ringwood. The double carriage-way was under construction. Beyond the old road I saw the scar made for the new : a huge gash cut in the gravel bank, stretching away rose-red in the evening light over the moorlands, so broad that for one awful moment I thought it had taken in the whole historic hollow and swept away the Rufus Stone itself.

The fear was soon allayed. To the north, beyond the gravel ridge, the secondary road dropped down to the woods through the familiar tangle of furze and stunted trees. The hollow was safe.

II

THE SCENE OF THE KILLING

I LEFT the car at the Rufus Stone and, crossing the road, made my way eastward about fifty yards to the summit of a small knoll amid the trees. There has been some felling and clearing here in relatively modern times, rather spoiling the ancient appearance but providing a convenient observation-post from which to view the immediate vicinity of the Stone.

From this point the first thing to strike me was that the number of trees in the area, in particular along the road back to the moorland ridge, had decreased considerably since the days of my boyhood. I did not have to rely upon memory, the fact is confirmed by the older maps and also by photographs. In my childhood one came down from the gorse and heather on the ridge by a steep track, no more than a bridle-path, leading north through a grove. The trees in the grove were widely spaced and of no great size, with little on the ground between them other than thin bracken, tufts of holly and coarse grass. It was, nonetheless, a grove.

Of course, some of the trees had to go when the modern road was first laid and then widened. Others—whose snaking roots can still be discerned, though the stumps have gone—may well have succumbed to old age; but in that case one would expect seedlings to have sprung, saplings to have grown, as they have in nearby woods. Since none exist, there can be little doubt that over the past fifty years the laying bare of the area to the south and south-east of the Stone has been caused, not only by the trampling of an ever-increasing number of sightseers, but still more by the parking, shunting and turning of countless motor vehicles. From this area the thin topsoil has long since been rubbed away, leaving a bald surface of hard-packed clay and gravel upon

18

which, the Forestry Commission agrees, natural regeneration is impossible. Of perhaps a score of trees known to have stood in the grove within living memory only a small clump remains. Fortunately it stands close to the Stone, which would otherwise be left in meaningless isolation.

But this regrettable denudation did not concern me just then. On this first day of the investigation my thoughts were not to be distracted by details that would only assume their relative importance much later. One point alone had now to be considered. Does the Rufus Stone really mark the site of the King's death, within a few feet either way? Can it be *proved*, with the degree of certainty demanded by historians? Unless, after an inquiry conducted with scrupulous fairness, I could give an affirmative answer I had far better admit failure, pack up and go home.

Long before setting out I had jotted down in my notebook the various reasons for and against the site. I have amplified these jottings below, at the same time rearranging them so that starting from the outside, geographically speaking, the argument works in towards the centre at the Stone itself, First, the documentary evidence.

Of this there is very little—a fact that has caused many a would-be searcher after the truth to give up prematurely—yet some valuable internal evidence is to be found in the various accounts of early chroniclers. Thus it can be regarded as certain, first, that the King was killed not in any other of the numerous forests of southern England, as is sometimes suggested, but in the New Forest; and, second, that because of the time-factor—of overriding importance, it will be seen—the place where he was killed lay not more than twenty miles from Winchester. The reasons for this second assumption will be examined later, but accepting it for the time being as true it will be seen that it limits the area in which the place is to be found to the north-eastern corner of the Forest.

If thereafter the early chroniclers fail to point to the exact spot it is almost certainly because, even if they knew it, they did not know how to identify it in the sparsely populated and, to them, unfamiliar wilderness. Some thirty-five years after the event Geoffrey Gaimar wrote—and I quote the old French so that there shall be no mistake—'*li reis estoit ale chacer vers Brokehest*'. Of this the only word to remain unchanged across the centuries is that indicative '*vers*'. It was the best he could do. Aware—or so it appears from his account—that the hunting party had originally set out from Winchester, to which it returned immediately after the King's death, he wanted to give some idea of where it had hunted but, unacquainted with the mazy Forest, the only place he could name was 'Brokehest'—so called in the Domesday survey—the one hamlet in the central Forest with a church.

From this phrase of Geoffrey Gaimar's later historians were to deduce, by giving the word '*vers*' a good stretching, that the King was killed 'near' Brokenhurst. But even if one accepts the preposition, how far is 'near'? In the two hundred-odd square miles of afforested land a distance of seven miles might with reason be called 'near'—as it is to this day in many an English rural postal address—and seven miles is the bee-line distance from Brockenhurst (Domesday church) to the Rufus Stone. On the other hand, it is surely quite unreasonable to transform 'near', as one modern historian does, into 'at'; he might as well say that the battle of Waterloo, fought near Brussels, was fought at Brussels. In any case, what rules out the vicinity of Brockenhurst is that it lies well beyond the maximum limit of twenty miles from Winchester imposed by internal evidence.

But did the man who told Gaimar really mean what Gaimar thought he meant? *Brokehest*, despite the Domesday reference, is not necessarily Brockenhurst. Nor is it certain that 'badger' is the correct rendering of *broke*, a word of Celtic origin whose use here seems a little unlikely in a region so long inhabited by Saxons. In fact the Anglo-Saxon words, usually given as *bróc* and *hyrst*, mean simply 'brook' and 'wood', and less than a mile to the north-west of the Rufus Stone, on the edge of what was later to become Brook Common, lies Brook Wood. In Norman times, given the scarcity of woodland names before the inclosures were

made, the designation may well have covered the adjacent area
to the south through which run two small converging streams
(now known as the King's Garn and Coalmeer Gutters), so that
the undefined boundary of the Brook Wood quite possibly merged
with that of the smaller wood, then unnamed, in which Rufus
was killed. Thus, standing at Malwood lodge, a man of the Walk
when asked some time after the event in which direction the King
had gone hunting might easily reply, in the absence of other
landmarks: 'Over there, towards *bróc-hyrst*.' No more than a
theory, it offers a reasonable alternative to the hamlet seven miles
away, which Gaimar and later historians perhaps too readily
accepted.

After Gaimar's pointer one has to wait a very long time before
finding anything of value. Most of the subsequent chroniclers,
when it comes to the death of Rufus, do little else than repeat
the accounts of their predecessors with embellishments based on
folklore, superstition and unverifiable legends. Not until Tudor
times is a new place-name given, and its chief interest then may
seem to reside in the proof it affords that in the Forest the event
was still remembered and the place known. Leland, travelling
through southern England and writing his *Itinerary*, quoted by
J. R. Wise, reported hearing that the King was killed at 'Thorough-
ham'—by which he meant the 'Truham' of Domesday Book, and
Truham (or Thruham) is Fritham.

This is not so positive as it sounds, because it is not easy to be
'at' Fritham at all since it is, or was, more of an area than a
place. It consists of an ancient tract of fertile land, contained
within a rough circle about three-quarters of a mile in diameter,
in which are scattered a number of farms and cottages, so that
a recognizable centre can scarcely be said to exist. But it is worth
noting that the most easterly of the houses that are said to be 'at'
Fritham stand within two miles of the Rufus Stone; further, that
the name is continued to the south over Fritham Plain which
runs up to Stoney Cross. And the eastern slope of this Plain lies
less than a mile to the west of the Stone and plays a part, though a
very small one, in the story of the King's death. Thus, a forest

dweller in the 16th century answering, perhaps at some distance from the spot, the inquiry of a passing stranger might easily say, inaccurately but for want of a better place-name, that the King fell at or near by Fritham.[1]

That Malwood was not mentioned by any of the early chroniclers is hardly surprising, because when they wrote, the name even if coined had not yet been given currency. From internal evidence, however, two primary conditions govern the approximate location of the hunting lodge at which the King and his party were staying up to the time of his death. Both are conditions of distance and both are fulfilled by Malwood. First, the place stands roughly nineteen miles by road from Winchester; secondly, it is less than a mile from the Rufus Stone. The distances themselves are governed by time, which will have to be examined closely later on; meanwhile they provide useful pointers that help to narrow down the search.

When, however, it comes to a pinpoint location of the spot where Rufus died, it has to be admitted that there is no early documentary evidence whatever. Nothing can be found other than oral tradition. And in the ordinary way such tradition is quicksand to the historian; at the first step forward he finds substance without solid foundation; at the second he sinks into a morass of romantic legend, unreliable gossip and sheer invention. But this is no ordinary tradition. To begin with it has the strength of simplicity. It does not attempt to pass on some complicated Arthurian fairy-tale; it states, clearly and as a fact, that the Rufus Stone marks the spot where stood a certain oak-tree. Details have been added by other voices : the glancing arrow, the chance bowshot of 'Sir Walter Tyrrell'. The firm voice of enduring tradition asserts only that here the King fell dead.

It goes without saying that those who handed down this tradi-

---

[1] I am indebted to Mr Jack Hargreaves, the television broadcaster, for the information that New Forest gypsies have a tradition that the King 'was not killed where that little bit of stone is, he was killed up on Fritham Plain.' This to some extent confirms Leland's report, but although it is never wise to scoff at gypsy traditions, this one they can only have received, at best, at second hand. There were no gypsies in the New Forest in the year 1100.

tion from generation to generation were men of the Forest, as unchanging as their native wilderness. Even now in an age of con-
fused acceleration they remain much as they were centuries ago :
West Saxons in appearance and in character, living long but saying
little, not to be stampeded into hasty action, slow to smile, reticent;
true descendants of that little world so long isolated under forest
law. Some change has, of course, been forced upon them; the
coming of the motor car, and even more of the motor coach, the
disturbances of two wars and the ever-louder calls of commerce
and industry have all affected their outlook and their way of life.
To get some idea of their knowledge of the past and of their ability
to hand down this knowledge with a reasonable degree of
accuracy it is necessary to consult those of the Forest historians
who examined the problem before the changes began to occur.

From one of these authorities a passage is worth quoting here.
The author : C. J. Cornish. The book : *The New Forest*, a well-
informed little volume first published in 1894, revised and re-
printed in 1910. The dates are mentioned because, from them,
Cornish is seen to be not only a near-contemporary—whose views
can be confirmed by many still living in the Forest today—but
also one observing and questioning in that bygone age at the close
of the 19th century when the customs and way of life of native
foresters were still those of a far more distant past. This is what he
wrote :

The evidence as to the exact place of the King's death does not
depend on history or upon general tradition. It is fixed by a con-
current and very coherent, though independent, set of circumstances. In the first place, by the fact . . . that by the fixed and
unchanging order of the Forest there have lived in continued
succession, within ten minutes ride of the place, persons employed
for 800 years to traverse daily that particular part of the
Forest, Malwood Walk, in the exercise of the same duty, the
supervision of the deer and the wood, men to whom by the very
nature of their business every tree, rivulet and pool is a familiar
object, frequently associated with some fact, far less important,
such as the death of an eagle or the leap of a deer, which is part
of the ordinary knowledge of the wood transmitted from one

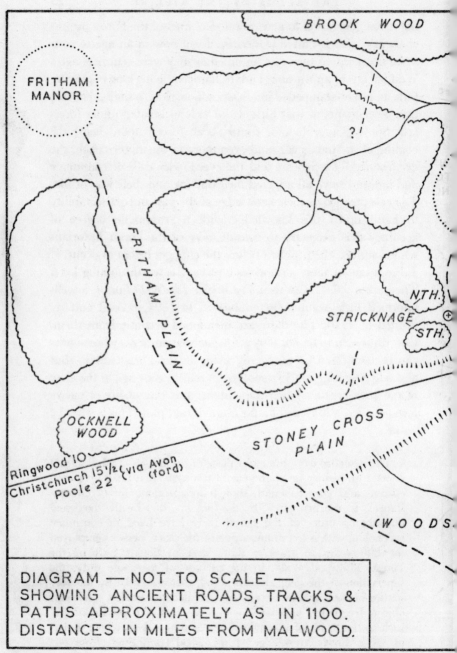

BROOK WOOD

FRITHAM
MANOR

?

FRITHAM PLAIN

NTH.

STRICKNAGE

STH.

⊕

OCKNELL
WOOD

STONEY CROSS
PLAIN

Ringwood 10
Christchurch 15½ (via Avon
Poole 22 (ford)

(WOODS.

DIAGRAM — NOT TO SCALE —
SHOWING ANCIENT ROADS, TRACKS &
PATHS APPROXIMATELY AS IN 1100.
DISTANCES IN MILES FROM MALWOOD.

Sketch map only.

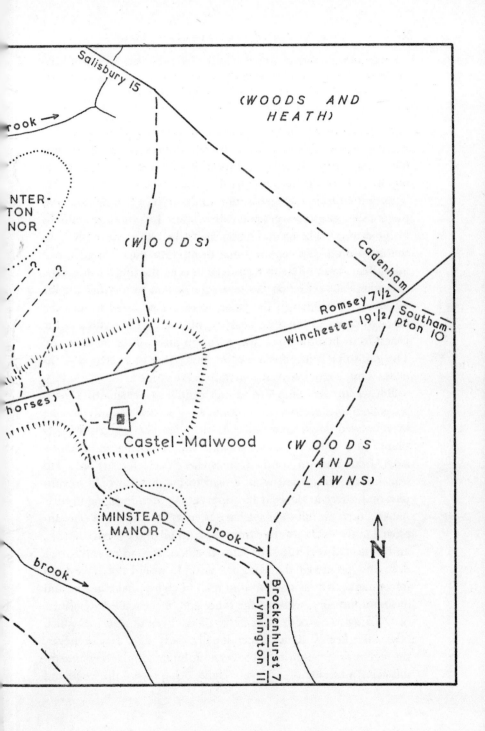

generation of foresters to the next. Secondly, the spot originally marked by an oak-tree was again marked by a stone, set up by Lord Delaware, then warden of the Forest, in 1745.

So factual an argument certainly strengthens the case for accepting the oral tradition. I found myself wondering, however, just how many men, in the Malwood Walk succession, would be required to cover the considerable distance of eight centuries. Transmitted from 'one generation to the next', Cornish said; and the usually accepted average is rather more than three generations to the century. The chain linking the early 12th to the early 20th century would thus require some twenty-five men. Enough, one might fear, to mutilate in transmission even the simplest message.

A moment's reflection, however, shows that twenty-five are far too many. The men in the chain were not required to pass the message down to the 20th century, but only to the 18th, to the year 1745 when the Stone was set up in place of the ancient oak. The gap to be bridged is not eight, but rather more than six centuries. Only some nineteen generations are needed.

But we are not compelled to stick rigidly to a calculation based on 'generations'. Indeed the probability of an oral tradition having been handed down from father to son is less likely, given the possibility of a break in the succession, than a passing on of knowledge from man to youth, from some elderly forester to a lad learning the job; a lad who, grown to manhood, would in turn pass on his lore to the next boy-apprentice. Men live long in their native Forest; it must always have been so, for the life of one employed in the Walk was free from the turmoil of the events outside, and protected within by the Crown, since he guarded the King's deer and preserved the King's woods. It would not have been uncommon, then as now, to find men of eighty, hale, hearty and of sound memory, while at the other end of the scale the business of 'walking' the woods must always have been of a sort to which boys take keenly at an exceptionally early age. It can never, throughout the centuries, have been unusual to find a boy of eight following a forester of, say, sixty-eight; being shown the woodland paths, the thickets where lay the deer, the trees that served as landmarks—and one tree in particular. It is even permissible, given the known life-span of many a native forester, to allow the man a greater age: say seventy-five, or more. Safer to stick at seventy for the man, ten for the boy, giving a mean age-gap of sixty years.

From sixty years to sixty years across the centuries, from an eye-witness surviving into the later years of the 12th to a young man in the early years of the 18th century would require rather more than ten men. Say ten men and a boy: a number small enough to warrant the belief that the message they handed down was not garbled on the way. But what converts the belief to something approaching certainty is the consideration that there must have been many more than one line of ten men. That from all the men of the Walk, the keeper and his numerous hunt-servants, who, in the evening of August 2nd 1100, saw the King's body at their feet, there may well have come a dozen lines of men to receive and to pass on the simple statement of fact: the fact that here had occurred the one notable event in English history of which they had personal knowledge. When it came to Lord Delaware in 1745, there must have been many inheritors of the ancient tradition ready to declare that knowledge before he decided, as the responsible representative of the Crown, to mark the site of the oak-tree beneath whose branches the King had fallen. And thinking back to those many ancestors who, at the time of the tragedy, must have known the exact spot of the King's death with certainty, it struck me forcibly that it would have been much more remarkable, incredible even, if their descendants in the unchanging Forest, instead of remembering the place, had forgotten it.

Before allowing myself to decide once and for all in favour of the Rufus Stone as the site of the King's death, I felt in duty bound to examine the evidence against it. Evidence? It is more a matter of doubt, honest but inarticulate. The doubters, generally at a distance, sometimes after viewing the Stone, merely shrug and turn away. One can only wish they would say something;

advance some fact that might be proved or disproved. For it is proof we want, not doubt, nor faith.

What do the native foresters say? One may leave out of account those few of Minstead and Stoney Cross and Canterton; for as long as they survive nothing will ever shake them from their firm belief. But what of the others elsewhere, those whose families have lived in the Forest undisturbed for centuries? Do they deny that the Rufus Stone marks the exact spot? I can only say that I have never met any to suggest—not, that is, with the smallest grain of supporting evidence—that the King died at some other place. Ancient tradition has it that when Ocknell Pond runs red it is because there the King's assassin washed bloodstained hands on his flight to the west. But, whether the 'blood' comes from the likely presence of iron in the water or from some minute algae, no one ever deduces from it that the King died in Ocknell Wood; on the contrary, the legend is used to support the belief that the King fell where he is said to have fallen. Farther afield, no native forester, so far as I know, seriously claims that Rufus was killed at or 'near' Brockenhurst; and the recent suggestion that he was done to death conveniently close to the motor museum at Beaulieu is not to be taken seriously. There is, of course, some ignorance of the subject, some silence; but all those who speak seem to echo the voices of those ten men and a boy. I have found nothing and no one to weaken the firm assurance of the oral tradition.

The documentary evidence, slender though it is, has thus yielded four localities that can be found on the map. With their approximate distances from the Rufus Stone, they are:

Winchester—20 miles (a maximum radius governed by time)
Fritham (south-east corner)—2 miles
Fritham Plain (eastern slope)—1 mile
'brokehest' meaning Brockenhurst—7 miles (from Domesday church)
'bróc-hyrst' meaning Brook Wood—$\frac{3}{4}$ of a mile.

Of these the best one can say is that taken together they contribute some geographical reality to the firm oral tradition naming the site, to which may be added the minor but equally ancient traditions naming Malwood half a mile to the east and Ocknell Pond a mile and a half to the west. From further evidence, to be examined later on, it will be seen that a Forest place-name, known of old but now almost forgotten, narrows the search to a very small area and that this area contains features exactly corresponding to a number of descriptive references supplied by several chroniclers.

When all these pointers, documentary, circumstantial or traditional, are examined in conjunction with the events known to have occurred in the evening of August 2nd, 1100, it will, I believe, be agreed that the exactness of the site of the Stone has been proved. And proved so surely that here and only here can the killing of the King have taken place.

III

EIGHT MEN AND THE KING

BEFORE continuing my investigations in the vicinity of the Rufus Stone I thought it best to take a closer look at Malwood. The place has a certain, though limited importance in the story of the King's death, but it has been somewhat neglected in the past and the fact that little is known about it inevitably makes one want to know more. To begin with, its name: Castle Malwood.

Were there no other evidence to prove its existence, the word 'castle' would have very little meaning; for there are a number of places in the Forest known as 'castles' that have no association with any building or fortification, where the name has been suggested by nothing more than some natural formation of the ground. At Malwood, however, a mound enclosed by well-marked earthworks proves that some building stood here in ancient times, almost certainly in those of the Conqueror, perhaps before him in the days of Edward or of Cnut. Further, it is known that a hunting lodge existed from the late Middle Ages onward, for when Forest records first begin to make their appearance the name of Malwood, as that of a 'lodge', occurs along with those, equally old, of Burley, Denny, Ashurst and others, from which it is invariably distinguished by the addition of 'castle' or 'keep'. Thereafter the names remain immutable throughout the centuries, denoting the headquarters of those keepers whose duty it was to patrol the 'walks': Malwood Walk, Ladycross Walk and so on.

In the mid-19th century the Deer Removal Act—which, intending total extermination, fortunately failed of its purpose—made redundant all the old Lodges from which the Walks were patrolled. Crown leases were then granted to wealthy tenants who, pulling down the primitive dwellings, built modern country-houses that effectively erased all traces of the past. Thus nothing remains of the earlier Malwood save the mound with the curving trench about it—though it is sometimes said in Minstead, or used to be in my boyhood, that part of the church was built of stone taken in the late 12th or early 13th century from the keep abandoned after the death of Rufus.

The fact that a lodge stood here in medieval times supports the strong local tradition, again uncontradicted by any other Forest claims, that this was the place where Rufus stayed and that, consisting of a Norman motte-and-bailey, it was termed a *'castel'*. Numerous advantages inherent in its situation confirm this view. Although lying well within the Forest, it is only nineteen miles from Winchester and no more than ten from Southampton, a handy port should the King wish—as on at least one occasion he did—to leave for Normandy at short notice. And communications in all other directions must have seemed exceptionally good in Norman times, what with the Winchester road no more than a couple of hundred yards away—a road prolonged to the west, to the Avon at Ringwood and so on to Poole or down to Christchurch—and a track leading north through the woods to the Salisbury road, and another running south, downhill to the ancient road that drove straight through the Forest to the Solent at Lymington. On high ground dominating the neighbourhood, with a spring nearby and the pastures of Minstead below, this was the ideal site for a royal hunting-lodge. No other lodge or manor-house then in existence in the New Forest can have possessed the same advantages, nor can any of them have been large enough to accommodate the King and his hunting-court.

Quite possibly it was built by the Conqueror himself soon after the afforestation decree in 1079; a primitive place, fortified for his personal security and royal dignity. Perhaps when Rufus took it over some improvements were made; perhaps he grumbled about it as he grumbled about the palace at Westminster built for him by Flambard and made some heavily humorous remark of disparagement, calling it a *'castel malvoute'*, much as in the revolt of 1095 he had called the tower erected to threaten Bamburgh a *'castel malvoisin'* ('bad neighbour castle'). And to the local West Saxons, habitually making a 'w' of a 'v', *voute* would sound like a word from their own tongue, the Anglo-Saxon *wudu*; the *'mal*-wood' they may have called it. Yet, since no early chronicler mentions the name, it may seem unlikely that it was formed until after Rufus was dead, when perhaps some Norman knight-huntsman declared his belief that the whole Walk was *mal*—evil.

But if the origin of the name is a matter of guesswork, what appears to be certain is that here, at the only *castel*-lodge in this part of the Forest, the King was staying shortly before his death. One may depict the sort of place it must have been, both from local conditions of topography and from the description of a similar hunting-lodge built in Northamptonshire some ninety years later for Richard I.[1] At Malwood the still discernible trench surrounding the whole of what was once the bailey forms an irregular square with rounded corners, the length of whose sides varies from 110 to 140 yards, enclosing an area of some $3\frac{1}{4}$ acres.[2] The necessary palisade to keep to keep out foxes, wolves and wild boar no longer survives, but it must have been raised upon the inner, higher side of the ditch. Towards the centre of the inclosure, upon the highest ground, the motte, stood the *castel*, part timber, part Purbeck stone and measuring perhaps fifty feet square. It was built on two low floors, with a large central hall on the main, upper floor, off which were chambers for the King, alcoves and cubicles for persons of importance, nooks and crannies for their attendants. On the ground floor, as well as sleeping quarters for the King's staff, were the armoury and guardroom, food and wine stores, and the kitchen with ovens using charcoal, efficient as a fuel and lessening both the smoke-nuisance and the fire-risk from flying sparks.

[1] The description is quoted in A. L. Poole's *From Domesday Book to Magna Carta*.
[2] Measurement taken from OS NG 1 : 2500.

On the slightly lower ground about the *castel*, the bailey held the stables and the thatched cottages of wattle-and-daub for the grooms and hunt servants. The kennels contained the 'tufters', that worked singly to find in dense cover, and the free-running hounds used to bring down wounded deer in the open; in all perhaps fifteen couple. There appear to have been two entrances to the inclosure, one on the east side, the other on the west; near each would be a guard-house, with a jail for defaulters or luckless offenders against the forest laws.

The King's household was of some size, even upon an informal hunting expedition. Nothing like so large, of course, as the itinerant court that normally accompanied him wherever he went—on those regular journeys, for instance, to Westminster, Gloucester and Winchester, where three times a year, at Christmas, Easter and Whitsun, following the example of his father he 'held court and wore his crown', or on other frequent travels to Windsor and Salisbury, or westward to Wales or north to Scotland. A court that, with its vast retinue of great men, their servants, wives and wenches, its clerical hangers-on and its powerful escort of mercenary troops, seemed to the unhappy people over whose land it passed and whose produce it consumed as terrible as a new army of conquest. By contrast the relatively small and, in the Forest at so short a distance from Winchester, almost self-supporting hunting-court would surely be welcomed by those foresters whose sole occupation was the hunting of deer, in which, however, they could only take part when the King was present.

The numbers required in the hunting-court household may roughly be estimated from the various posts to be filled and jobs to be done. The Steward was in charge of the 'hall' at the *castel*, together with its larder, pantry and other offices, each with its 'master dispenser'. In charge of the King's chamber was the Chamberlain, whose staff included the bearer of the King's bed, the ewerer who attended to the King's ablutions, the tailor who looked after the King's wardrobe, and the King's barber. The Butler had charge of all wines, his staff including cupbearers, cellarers and fruiterers, and the King also had his personal cup-bearer or *dapifer*, an official of high rank. In addition, below stairs, there would of course be cooks, scullions and other menials; so that in all one may guess at a total indoors of some forty to fifty men. Outdoors, the Constable was in charge of the stables where the lads had in their care the large number of riding-horses as well as pack animals and carthorses, with carters to look after the carts for baggage. The Marshal was responsible for order and discipline throughout the court, and also controlled the bodyguard of mounted men-at-arms numbering, at a guess, from fifty to perhaps one hundred. The grand total of this small hunting-court may thus have amounted to some one hundred and fifty to two hundred men.

Assembled at the *castel*, some of them living there permanently, would be the Chief Hunter, the other knight-huntsmen and numerous hunt servants, as well as the keeper of the Walk and his men. Also present, if only for the duration of the King's visit, would be some of those responsible for the upkeep of the Forest and the application of its laws. Assuming these various officials and local men to have numbered perhaps fifty, it would appear that over two hundred persons were gathered temporarily in or about the *castel* and its bailey. The King and each of his guests would, of course, be accompanied by at least one personal attend-ant, a man of junior rank to look after his equipment and his weapons—call him an *écuyer*, for the later 'esquire', but the pre-cise title is of no consequence here. Since the chroniclers nowhere mention women in the hunting party, we may assume there were none.

It seems probable that the greater part of the household, taking with it the baggage and the King's furniture on pack-horses or in carts, would set out from Winchester in the morning of the day named by the King, so as to make sure that the *castel* was ready for occupation that night. The royal party, escorted by the body-guard, would follow later in the day or whenever the King chose to move. A leisurely progress; for it is essential to forget the idea, inspired by romantic fiction, that men once on horseback were forever dashing about the countryside at full gallop. In fact it seems improbable that in Norman times any horseman ever allowed his mount to gallop at all if he could help it. Exhausting to both horse and rider, it was also dangerous. The old Roman highways apart, the winding roads—no better than rough tracks running for the most part through heavily wooded country —were rutted in the open, and miry beneath the trees, whose overhanging branches and snaking roots presented a recurrent double peril; and no one can then have forgotten either the mortal injury suffered by the Conqueror in Mantes only thirteen years previously, or the earlier riding accident that had killed his second son Richard in the Forest. With cumbersome harness and furnishings, with a saddle uncomfortable in the extreme, built upon a massive framework that terminated in a high iron pommel, a fall at speed, even a stumble, might prove fatal.

Nor must the other compelling reason for a generally slow rate of progress be forgotten. The horse then in use, principally the Norman percheron, was certainly capable of carrying, at a steady gait and over relatively long distances, the considerable weight of an armed and heavily equipped rider; and the royal bodyguard, bearing sword and bow, would be wearing chain-mail and iron helmets. But its best pace was the walk, roughly eight miles an hour. Urged to a trot its speed would rise to ten, at best to twelve; in an emergency and forced to a lumbering canter,[1] a maximum of fifteen miles might possibly be covered in the hour. But this total, if it was ever reached, can never have been exceeded. A journey at that pace might be prolonged with the help of led horses to serve as remounts, but not indefinitely; the horses could not make it, and no large relays of fresh horses would normally be available. A royal cavalcade, moreover, had to be kept together and its speed was therefore that of its slowest members. For the horses of the heavily accoutred bodyguard a distance of

[1] That the English had not yet coined the word 'canter' seems to show that the gait was at least unusual. It must still have been novel a couple of centuries later when, riding a lighter breed of horse, the pilgrims to Becket's shrine set the fashion of the canter to Canterbury.

fifteen miles within the hour would seem to be beyond the accepted limit of endurance.

The King, however, would have no cause for hurry. Time and the land were his; there was no need to suffer discomfort or court danger. So it seems safe to say that—walking, sometimes trotting, occasionally halting—the average pace would hardly exceed the steady eight miles an hour of the walk, and that the twenty-mile journey between Winchester and the *castel* at Malwood would normally take some two and a half hours, perhaps more if a halt were made at Romsey. But it is important to remember in view of subsequent events that, even at the utmost speed possible, the twenty miles could not be covered in less than an hour and a half.[1]

And so one fine afternoon at the end of July the royal hunting party, over a hundred strong in all, came up the ancient road between the trees from Cadenham. 'Fine' for three reasons: if the weather had been bad the King would not have started at all; had there been heavy rain or thunder the chroniclers would surely have mentioned such obvious portents of disaster; and the sun certainly shone in the evening of August 2nd. At 'the end of July', because when the chroniclers come to relate the events leading up to the King's death they have him dining and staying the night at the *castel* on August 1st, without the least hint that he had only just arrived, which seems to indicate that he had already been there for a day or two.[2] On the other hand, he would not have come to the Forest until after July 20th, since before that was the close-season for deer hunting, the 'Fence Month' when the does were calving.

Even at a walk, the hoof-beats of so large a cavalcade would

---

[1] This estimate, as well as the foregoing passage on horsemanship in Norman times, has been confirmed by two authorities consulted independently. Fifteen miles in the hour is still the accepted maximum for a ridden horse.

[2] The Sunday previous to his death was the feast of St Peter-ad-Vinculam. Rufus, who for all his scoffing did not habitually stay away from church, may have attended Mass that morning at Winchester and have set out for the Forest soon afterwards. This would give three clear days' hunting before the fatal Thursday.

be audible at some distance in the quiet woods. The watch at the inclosure's eastern entrance would give a warning shout; the guard, turning out, would throw open the gate in the palisade as the vanguard appeared; the officials of the alerted household would hasten from the *castel*; and, as the King rode in, the foresters and hunt servants would come running to fall on their knees before him. Perhaps to their humble greeting, the King riding on—bullet-headed, rubicund, shorter than his tremendous father but equally deep-chested and broad of girth—returned some gruffly cheerful reply. Though he could threaten fiercely enough, to those who served him loyally he was a good-humoured master and, away from the ceremony of State occasions, seldom stood upon his dignity. Now in the prime of vigorous life, a bachelor of no more than forty-three and at the height of his power and fame, he was the unchallenged monarch of all he surveyed in England and of much else besides. Ruler of Normandy by right of treaty during his brother Robert's absence on crusade, Count of Maine by right of conquest, with great plans for the future shortly to mature, plans evolved in secret with the Duke of Aquitaine, here in the Forest, about to enjoy the pleasures of hunting, he could afford to relax. Perhaps he relaxed too much.

Behind him and to either side rode his companions.

First his brother, Count Henry, ten years his junior; smooth-faced, sharp-eyed, a fringe of dark-brown hair hiding his forehead; also a bachelor, but with a number of strumpet-mistresses and a greater number of bastards; a sly fellow, landless but wealthy. Next, Robert fitz-Hamon, perhaps the King's oldest and closest friend, among the few to support him against the rebellious barons stirred up by Odo, Earl-Bishop of Bayeux, in 1088, and who supported him again in 1095. Holding lands in Oxfordshire, wisely and justly administered, more recently he had successfully invaded south Wales, thrusting into Glamorgan to found Cardiff Castle. A man of unswerving loyalty.

Next in line there may well have ridden a trio: Earl Gilbert and his brother Roger of the great house of Clare, and the man who, some fifteen years previously, had married their youngest sister Adelice (Alice); Walter Tirel of Poix—holder of considerable lands in Ponthieu and enfeoffed on marriage by his late father-in-law, Count Richard Clare de Bienfaite de Tunbridge who had fought at Hastings, with the manor of Langham in Essex (Domesday: Laingaham). Friends of the King, the Clares seem to have been even more the friends of Henry; Tirel, on the other hand, was 'a stranger at court' (Gaimar).

After them in the cavalcade there rode another trio: the Norman barons Gilbert de Laigle and William de Monfichet and, a somewhat older man, William of Breteuil, son of William fitz-Osbern, one in whom the King placed great trust since he was Keeper of the Treasury in Winchester—of the Treasure that included, as well as crown, sword and jewelled sceptre, the ceremonial robes and dalmatics, the hoard of gold and silver, that most priceless treasure of all, the *Liber de Thesauro*, inventory of the King's possessions in England, the great Domesday Book and its kindred surveys.

So they rode in, on one of those last days of July; rode through the inclosure and up to the *castel*-lodge; eight great men behind their bluff, authoritative, confident King.

IV

THREE MEN AND THE CROWN

T
HE present inquiry is no place for a full-length biography of William Rufus, or of either of his brothers for that matter. But if one is to find out how a man died, it is a good thing to find out first how he lived. What sort of a man was he? What did he do? Who were his friends, who his enemies? Some of the answers must be given here if the mystery of his death is to be solved.

First, his name. 'Rufus' it is to English-speaking people and always will be; yet it is unlikely that he was ever called that by his contemporaries. True, once or twice the chroniclers in their Latin texts refer to him as *'Wilhelmus Rufus'*. But Latin was not what his companions spoke. What they called him then, though not invariably and not presumably to his face, was what in France they call him still: *le roux*, or in the ancient tongue used by Geoffrey Gaimar *li rei rus*. And it is worth remembering that *le roux* and *le rouquin* are common French nicknames more often endearing than disparaging.

But if it was the medieval chroniclers who started the habit, it was E. A. Freeman who, in the mid-19th century with his *Reign of William Rufus*, gave the name a wider and more sinister currency. To Freeman, prejudiced champion of the Church and protagonist of an almost entirely imaginary Anglo-Saxon 'democracy', Rufus appeared as the very embodiment of all things wicked, a tyrant so horrible that to paint him black was not enough. Freeman chose red. In the pages of his biography the mere chance that the King had a florid complexion and reddish hair is turned against him as the outward symbol of an inner and unspeakable depravity. Red: the colour of the blood he spilled, of the deer he hunted, of the devil himself and the flames of hell to which Freeman, self-appointed spokesman for the Almighty, consigned him in 'eternal damnation'.

In the end of course it was Freeman who was damned. He went too far, and he knew it. Finding, rather reluctantly, that Rufus had some good points he confessed that he could not understand the subject of his biography at all. Which was not surprising to Dr Margaret Murray, who remarked that Freeman was 'no anthropologist'. She might almost have added : 'and no historian'; for by the end of his century he had been demolished, taken to pieces page by page in J. H. Round's famous essays in historical detection, collected in *Feudal England*. 'We see that in all these fantasies,' he wrote after dissecting some of Freeman's worst blunders concerning Rufus, 'we have what can only be termed history in masquerade.' And the reason for this, Round concluded, was that Freeman 'first formed an idea, and then, under its spell, fitted the facts to it without question.'

For one idea Freeman could find no facts at all, but that did not stop him from developing the thought and committing it to paper. To back his accusation there was not enough evidence to hang a cat, but the opportunity was too good to be missed. So Rufus was unmarried? Yet flaunted no mistresses, paraded no string of bastards! And did not his brother Henry, that notorious fornicator, profess to be shocked at the King's private life? The 'idea' was formed and 'under its spell' the answer appeared simple : Rufus was a sodomist. And since there is always some fun to be had by slinging that sort of mud from a safe distance, others were soon repeating Freeman's allegation of homosexuality as though it were proven fact. Not until Christopher Brooke's *Saxon and Norman Kings*, published in 1963, do we get a balanced judgment. 'There is no precise evidence in support of the charge . . . and historians who have followed Freeman in saying that "no mistresses . . . are mentioned or hinted at" are in error . . . If no children are recorded the probable explanation is either that the King could not beget children or that none grew up.' Alternatively, Rufus may have resembled his father more than his

younger brother; despite the licentiousness of what often seemed
more of a military camp than a regal court, he may have felt less
inclined than Henry to jump into bed with every available wench.

As Christopher Brooke wisely says: 'There is no case here for
whitewash.' But if one is to see Rufus at all clearly, some at least
of Freeman's red-paint daubing must be wiped off. What lies beneath? What, in the first place, do his critics the contemporary
chroniclers say in his favour?

William of Malmesbury: 'He was brave; he honoured his
father's memory; he could at times act wisely and with decision.'

Orderic Vitalis: 'He was imperious, daring and warlike, and
gloried in the pomp of his numerous troops. His memory was very
tenacious . . . and his efforts to keep the peace throughout his
dominions were unceasing.'

More poetically, Geoffrey Gaimar discusses a character of
'great nobility'.

Of all this Margaret Murray says that it 'shows the King as a
great man and a fine ruler', and she herself sees him as 'a dutiful
son—a faithful friend—recklessly courageous, lavishly open-
handed'.

Christopher Brooke perceives 'a shrewd mind, a ready wit . . .
to the narrow circle of his knights he was generous and honourable'.

In *The Feudal Kingdom of England (1042-1216)* Frank Barlow examines the King's character at greater length. Rufus, he
says, had 'little personal dignity . . . a simulated bluster and a
threatening countenance (did) service for the natural sternness and
gravity' of his father. Yet he had a 'clear conception of the majesty
of his office and neglected none of his duties'. His policy was
'soundly conceived'; he was 'greedy of money . . . but spent it to
good purpose'; he 'crushed his enemies with less chicanery than
his father had used and certainly with less savagery'; and 'the
Norman church was to welcome his strong rule and to think his
mocking jests a small price to pay for peace and order.' An important point, he 'never behaved unnaturally towards his kin'
and 'cherished always the memory of his parents'. There were in

the 11th century 'many monsters of cruelty . . . William II was
not amongst them . . . His generosity and chivalry, his innate good
nature, his fearless conduct were readily acclaimed by the knightly
class.'

When Barlow further reminds us that 'it was in the thirteen
years of his reign that the provisional contrivances of his father
were held fast and made firm' we are surely entitled to say that
here was a King who did his duty as he understood it and did
it well. And when the same author recalls that Rufus on his acces-
sion 'distributed his father's treasure to the churches and monas-
teries according to his father's Will—an action which left him
poor—and he restored his uncle, Bishop Odo of Bayeux, whom
the Conqueror's death had released from prison, to his earldom
of Kent—an action which threatened his security', we begin to
discover a man who, whatever the truth about his private life, was
not devoid of nobility, a man who kept faith, who was trusting
and ready to forgive and forget. Perhaps, concerning his brother
Henry, he forgave and forgot too much.

On the other side of the medal, A. L. Poole sees Rufus as
'cynical . . . ill-tempered . . . blasphemous'. Cynicism is apparent
in his retort to the reproach that certain reforms promised to the
Church had not been effected: 'What man can keep *all* of his
promises?'—which, however, is no more than our modern politi-
cians say, if they be honest, when reminded of their election
pledges. 'Ill-tempered'? Other recent historians say 'quick-tem-
pered'; probably with better reason, for the King's moments of
explosive wrath seem to have passed as quickly as they came and
not to have been followed by savage conduct. 'Blasphemous' con-
veys the impression of habitual foul-mouthed wickedness; yet the
instance generally quoted by the chroniclers—the King's swear-
ing 'by God's face' or 'by the face of Lucca', referring apparently
to some miraculous imprint of the face of Christ—was an oath
used only, says Margaret Murray, when he intended to be taken
seriously. It seems likely that Normans then swore with much the
same staunch profanity as their descendants do to this day and
that the King swore no harder than the rest. He was certainly

determined not to be dominated by the Church and, in asserting his authority, the use of strong language would come as naturally to him as to any man of his time. Perhaps, too, with his rough and irrepressible sense of humour, he rather enjoyed shocking young clerics too timid to protest, who in turn and secretly rather enjoyed being shocked.

Yet something of Freeman's fierce and unrelenting denunciation still seems to linger in the mind of the modern historian. How else account for the condemnation of Rufus made, without the disclosure of any new evidence, by so distinguished a scholar as A. L. Poole? 'From the moral standpoint he was probably the worst king that has occupied the throne of England.'

Which 'moral standpoint'? Ours—in the late 20th century? Freeman's in the late 19th? Or that of the Normans at the end of the 11th? And how do we judge by the changing standards of successive ages who, among the many bad, was 'the worst king'? There are, I submit, some half a dozen kings of England whose well-attested moral turpitude would, in any fairly conducted inquiry, make Rufus's allegedly immoral life appear almost saintly. In his own time, and far beyond England, Rufus was not depicted as either homosexual or common lecher; towards the close of his reign he was seen, in Normandy and in the royal demesne of France, as a mighty and victorious king and when he died men sang his praises and spoke of him with regret.

Moreover, had Freeman's dark hints of unspeakable vice, of gross and persistent debauchery had any solid foundation in fact, some evidence of premature decline, however slight, would surely have been visible as he grew older, some slowing of mental powers, an increase in cruelty, a falling off of good-humoured activity. And yet he was forty-two when there occurred an incident as sparkling as any in his spirited youth.

The story goes, as Gaimar tells it, that a messenger bringing news of the rebellion in Maine, led by Hélias of La Flèche in 1099, reached him in the New Forest while he was at dinner after a day's hunting. 'Comment va?' cried the King joyfully, bidding the man be seated at the table. Then, having listened to the bad news, he rose at once, mounted and rode off to Southampton to take ship for France. It was June and a gale was blowing—one that seems to have anticipated in its force that which battered the coasts of Normandy eight hundred and forty-five years later. Ordering his companions to follow on next day with the troops, he boarded a small vessel. The helmsman-skipper demurred: no one could sail in such weather; they would all be drowned, the King included. Laughing at his fears, Rufus shouted above the wind: 'I never yet heard tell of a king who was drowned—and you can be sure I'll not be the first. Shove off!'

Thus heartened the crew put to sea. How or where they passed the night is not told, but fortune certainly favoured Rufus's boldness. Landing next day upon the Normandy coast, at the mouth of the river Touques, safe but alone, he commandeered a horse—a priest's mare, it seems—rode to the castle of Bonneville and summoned a body of men. Thence, marching into Maine, he quelled the revolt at Le Mans promptly and without savagery. By Michaelmas he was back in England to resume his hunting.

It is hard to believe that any of this could have been achieved by the sort of man described by his more violent detractors: a pot-bellied dwarf, red with rage, besotted by evil living. The incident shows him as one fit in mind and body, a king who knew his job, a commander whose spirited example must, as such examples always do, have inspired respect in his companions and affection in the hearts of his soldiers. Nor is the incident isolated; he had shown the same prompt resolution, the same combination of boldness, skill and speed, in suppressing the rebellions in England of 1088 and 1095. Rebellions of which the Anglo-Saxon chronicler noted with true insular pride that it was the 'Frenchmen' who rebelled and the 'Englishmen' who stayed loyal; thereby proving the good sense of the English who preferred, to the cruel anarchy of ruthless and truculent barons, the firm rule of the King with its law, order and rough justice.

How is it then that this successful monarch who had thrust back the Welsh and pacified the Scots, who had held England together and rescued Normandy from anarchy and had ruled, Poole

admits, 'efficiently' in both countries, how is it that immediately
after his death he was so violently attacked by the ecclesiastics,
not abroad, but in his own kingdom? True, as Brooke says, 'the
Church was mainly hostile to Rufus before 1100, and with good
reason.' But the hostility was largely due to his methods of exact-
ing money; yet money he must have if he was to rule at all.

One of the Church's chief complaints concerned the 'reliefs'—
medieval equivalent of our infinitely heavier estate duties—pay-
able to the Crown by an heir before he could succeed to the
lands of a deceased tenant-in-chief. These the Church avoided by
claiming that for a bishop to pay reliefs to the King would savour
of simony—not a very honest argument since, as Poole says, the
venality of the church was notorious and the purchase of sees by
clerks at court was common practice. Rufus, however, with the
help of his much-maligned but supremely competent official
Ranulf Flambard—whom he later made Bishop of Durham where
he was regarded as a saint—got round the bishops' refusal to pay
by demanding the reliefs from their sub-tenants, which was certainly an abuse of feudal custom. But the alternative was even
more painful to the Church. Whenever an abbacy or a bishopric
fell vacant through the death of the holder the King, following
the earlier example of continental rulers, simply kept the office
vacant and collected the revenues for himself. When Anselm,
Archbishop of Canterbury *malgré lui*—a devout little man, full
of reforming zeal but difficult, who could never get on with either
Rufus or the Pope—asked whether some of the numerous vacant
abbacies might not be filled, the King retorted. 'What's that to
you? Aren't the abbeys all mine?' Which was unanswerable,
because they *were* his; abbots and bishops holding their tem-
poralities from the Crown just as lay tenants-in-chief held their
land.

And so the King blustered and swore; laughed, and collected
the cash. And the Church grumbled and groaned, but was not
ruined or anything like it; hurt in its pride more than its purse.
After all, as J. H. Round pointed out, the paying of reliefs was no
more a new custom introduced by Rufus than was the system of

military tenure; and abuses of established feudal custom committed by his contemporaries in Europe and his successors in
England were much the same and frequently worse. Nor were
the chroniclers unanimous in attacking the abuses during the
King's lifetime. The old Anglo-Saxon writer, for instance, pains-
takingly recording events year by year, more often than not links
his vague grousing against the King to more positive moans about
the weather : 'It rained all summer long and the taxes were very
oppressive . . . The crops were ruined by floods caused by inces-
sant rain and the taxation was heavy . . . What times we live in !'
From which one may gather that the dominant topics of English
conversation have scarcely changed across the centuries.

From the day of the King's death a very different note is
sounded. The Anglo-Saxon chronicler, reporting that Rufus was
'killed with an arrow, while hunting, by one of his men', goes on
to comment tersely 'he was hated by almost all his people'—
which is far from true—'and abhorrent to God'—which is no
more than the party-line toed henceforth and for many years to
come by other monkish chroniclers in England. The reason for
the campaign of disparagement seems clear. Bent on explaining
away the King's death so that the Church should not be involved
in a suspected crime, a crime whose author might be the man they
supported as successor to the throne, they attributed the removal
of the now 'abhorrent' Rufus to an act of God. It was simple and,
in a superstitious age, quite plausible to the masses.

The supposed hatred of 'all' the people does not stand up to
close scrutiny. The inarticulate English, 'oppressed and down-
trodden' under Rufus says Poole—but their case had been worse
under the Conqueror and was to be worse still under Henry—
had twice supported him to a man against the rebellious barons
and had answered the call to service in Normandy without undue
protest; though they certainly feared, they cannot have felt such
dread for him as they had for his father. At the other end of the
scale, the majority of the barons do not appear to have actively
hated him; towards the end of his reign it seems more than likely

that, had they been asked, they would have joined him in any enterprise he cared to name provided it brought them material advantage. As for the bishops, they too had supported him against the rebels—with the doubtful exception of William of Saint-Calais, the argumentative Bishop of Durham, and the obvious exception of the trouble-making Earl-Bishop Odo who, banished after the rebellion of 1095, had died peacefully enough at Palermo in 1097. The revenues lost by the Church to the King were a continuing source of annoyance; yet in the endless dispute with the Archbishop of Canterbury the 'tyranny' of Rufus 'was not enough', Frank Barlow notes, 'to produce one responsible supporter for Anselm's new ideas'. Many ecclesiastics must have perceived that redress for their grievances was improbable so long as Rufus lived; few can have been obsessed by such black detestation as to plot his murder.

But if the bishops did not plan it—supposing, ahead of proof, that it *was* murder, and not a hunting accident—who did? Neither the Norman barons as a class nor the mass of the English people stood to gain from the King's sudden death. To whom then would it be profitable? Before giving an answer, one must look more closely at the King's brothers.

V

ROBERT AND HENRY

O F Robert, born *circa* 1054, it is said that he was nick-
named 'curthose' because his legs were abnormally short.
Perhaps they were, for neither in appearance nor in
character did he resemble his father; but what in fact the name
implied is not so sure. The *courte heuse* which Robert seems to
have favoured were a sort of breeches, tight about the calf and
terminating well above the ankles, sometimes little below the
knee; whereas the more customary *heuse*, seen in the Bayeux
tapestry, usually went down to include the foot rather like a
dancer's tights and were worn with a light boot laced at the
ankle. The man who wore the unfashionable *courte heuse* might
be deemed eccentric; he was not necessarily a dwarf.

Undersized or not, what historians have often called him is
'despicable'—which seems inadequate. He had some good
qualities. He could be gentle, chivalrous, and on occasion displayed physical courage, endurance and skill. Yet, as rebellion
against his father had proved, he was headstrong and unreliable.
Almost worse in the long run, he was gullible, easily parted from
his money by those who pretended friendship and then turned
against him. In all, and despite his occasional rages, not a bad
fellow at heart, but certainly the last man to be burdened with
the responsibility of ruling the quarrelsome factions and turbulent
barons of Normandy. Trouble became inevitable from the day
when he assumed power.

The Conqueror upon his deathbed in Rouen must have known
it; yet he had seen no way of avoiding the break-up of that Anglo-
Norman unity he had been at such pains to achieve. Robert, for
all his rebellious folly, could not be deprived of his birthright.

The dukedom must be his. But not the kingdom. To hold England, to maintain the conquest, Rufus alone had the strength of character. Henry was too young; at nineteen his abilities were unknown, untested. Instead of land the dying Conqueror bequeathed him bullion.

One can hardly blame a man awaiting death in agony for failing to guard against all eventualities, but it would have been better had the Conqueror been able to pass on to Rufus some wise advice concerning Henry's future. Without that advice Rufus stuck faithfully to his father's last wishes, but never went beyond them. Throughout his reign he seems to have treated Henry with notable kindness. He forgave him his open defiance and his black misdeeds, permitted him to indulge his lascivious pleasures, took him campaigning and hunting and allowed him his rightful place at court. But he gave him no English land and no authority. Henry remained the younger brother; and, from his later performance, one may perceive the development of his character. Ambitious, frustrated, restless, with few outlets for his talents and energy save in the hunting field or the bedchamber, it is easy to imagine how the pressure built up over the years to the point of explosion. A grievance, however imaginary, darkened his thoughts. He believed he had a better right to the throne than either of his brothers.

It may be that Rufus would have acted differently had Henry not given clear proof, in 1091, of the course he would follow were he allowed greater independence. In that year, while Rufus and Robert were at daggers drawn in Normandy, he had snatched at power, seizing a number of castles together with a large part of the Cotentin peninsula and the island-fortress of Mont Saint-Michel. A shortlived triumph; his brothers, composing their quarrel, joined forces against him and, laying siege to Mont Saint-Michel, speedily compelled the surrender of all he had gained.

It was then that Rufus displayed, as well as political wisdom, his innate good nature. All past quarrels between him and his brothers were ended and mended. A treaty was negotiated by

D

which, in addition to a promise by Rufus to support Robert with military force, it was agreed that each of the two, the King and the Duke, should be the other's heir should either die childless. And, to cap this agreement that went some way to restoring the unity of England and Normandy, Rufus carried both Robert and Henry off to England whence he led them upon a congenial expedition against the Scots. For a while the outlook had seemed bright.

It had not perhaps seemed so bright to young Henry. The treaty clouded his future. Before its signing, with Rufus and Robert at loggerheads, he might reasonably hope that some day England would be his. Now Robert was the heir. And should Robert die childless, then Rufus got Normandy. For Henry there was nothing. He still held no land in England and his only prospect of gaining power lay in the possibility that both his brothers would die without issue. As time passed and brought no improvement he may well have brooded upon the humiliating uncertainties of his position, yet of the dark thoughts that may then have entered his mind he gave no sign. In Normandy an unpleasant streak of savagery had shown itself in his character, a liking of cruelty for cruelty's sake; in England such evil tendencies were repressed, submerged beneath the lust and the avarice for which he was becoming noted.

Occasionally some unexpected event must have brought him a surge of wild hope. As when Robert, unable to obtain the promised military support from Rufus, flew into a rage and denounced the treaty of friendship and inheritance. As when, in 1093, with Henry now the heir-apparent, Rufus fell gravely ill and lay for a while at death's door in Gloucester. Or as when, in 1094, Rufus, restored to vigorous health, invaded Normandy and proceeded to buy off the barons one by one—something Robert could no longer afford to do—rather than engage in a war of castle sieges and devastation; and with Robert ousted might not Henry expect eventually to inherit the dukedom? The process was interrupted in 1095 by rebellion in England; but in the following year there occurred a startling development across the

Channel, something that may, after initial consternation, have aroused in Henry's heart a more malignant hope.

Robert, caught up by the great wave of religious emotion then sweeping Christendom, had answered Pope Urban's call to the crusade. Unable to raise the funds necessary for such an expedition, he had offered Normandy in pawn to Rufus who, accepting the pledge, had advanced the cash. The brothers were reconciled, the treaty reaffirmed. Once again each was the other's heir; if Rufus died childless, Robert, retaining the dukedom, would succeed to the kingdom. Henry was out of the running, unless—and from this, surely, must have sprung the secret hope—unless Robert failed to return. More than a possibility, the perils of so great an adventure, the chances of shipwreck, of capture, of death in battle or through sickness, must have made it appear distinctly probable. Henry bided his time.

For three years he waited, watching Rufus go from strength to strength; from undisputed rule in England to unchallenged authority in Normandy; from victorious, if almost profitless war in the Vexin to undeniable triumph in Maine. Saw him grow in might and magnificence : king, duke, count, almost an emperor in the spread and variety of his dominions. Saw him hold his first court in the great new hall at Westminster where, by the custom introduced by his father, the coronation was re-enacted. Watched him, as Barlow sees him, moving in solemn procession behind the household officers, the bishops and the abbots, preceeded by Edgar, King of Scots, bearing the sword of state before his overlord. Saw the golden crown placed upon his head and the jewelled sceptre into his right hand, a resplendent figure surrounded by his barons, guarded by well-armed mercenary troops. A King, wrote Gaimar, whose 'great nobility made all men his servants.' And seeing him thus in majesty, Henry can hardly have escaped the bitter reflection that he, Henry, held only a castle in Normandy and the treasure his father had left him—that and the conditional inheritance, remote, improbable.

It may be that at some time during those three years he spoke to his confident, good-natured elder brother to ask for some recognition, some assurance for the future. Did Rufus then put him off with vague and jocular half-promises, coupled perhaps to the sharp reminder that his word was pledged to Robert and that, by God's face, he would keep his promise? At all events he did nothing to enhance his younger brother's status; Henry was heir-presumptive, no more. Thus, Rufus may unwittingly have kindled in Henry's restless thoughts a flame of unforgiving resentment.

For the rest there is no evidence; yet it is reasonable to suppose in view of what followed that at some time during those years of waiting, with Robert lost to sight beyond the eastern horizon, Henry discussed the grave if still distant uncertainties of the succession with some of the more learned clerics at court. What if the King should die? To sound opinion he may well have hinted that, whatever the treaty laid down, Robert Curthose was scarcely the man to wear the crown of England. If so, he can have been left in no doubt that, however strong his own claim, no man could expect to receive the Church's blessing who did not first promise to right the Church's grievances. With this in mind he may then have begun to consider a forestalling of the absent Robert.

Suddenly, like a peal of distant thunder, the news began to roll in. Robert was returning. In the campaign leading to the capture of Jerusalem he had distinguished himself by his chivalry and resourceful courage. On the way back he had stopped in Norman Apulia. There, aided by his new-found reputation, he had gained the hand of a delectable bride: Sybil, daughter of Geoffrey of Conversano who, a grandson of Tancred de Hauteville, was nephew both to the mighty Robert Guiscard, Duke of Apulia, and to Roger I, Great Count of Sicily. A highly profitable marriage, it had brought Robert Curthose a dowry more than sufficient to pay off the mortgage on Normandy. More significantly, the union held out the likely prospect of male issue, of a son who should be heir not only to the dukedom, but also to the throne of England.

Rufus seems to have taken the news with equanimity. With many useful irons in the fire and considerable military strength, it has been suggested that he was contemplating an attack upon Anjou to bring to heel its disagreeable and troublesome ruler, Count Foulk *le réchin*. On the other hand, although next to nothing is known of his negotiations with the young Duke William of Aquitaine, a deal similar to that made with Robert over Normandy may have been nearing a satisfactory conclusion. The Duke, an early troubadour romantic, more of a poet than a ruler and as impecunious as Robert, was off on a pilgrimage to the Holy Land; to raise the cash he was ready, Orderic Vitalis believes, to mortage his County of Poitou. The transaction would be made final before the end of the year in the Duke's capital; Rufus would go there to celebrate—'*à Poitiers ma fête tiendrai*' Geoffrey Gaimar makes him exclaim joyfully. The problem of Normandy could wait. Even if Robert did pay off his debt, it seems unlikely, modern historians agree, that Rufus would hand over control immediately, allowing the dukedom to sink back into near-anarchy under his brother's weak rule. Possibly he contemplated some form of condominium, with Robert sitting back to enjoy married life in affluence whilst he, Rufus, got on with the business of efficient administration. Perhaps—but this is no more than a guess for which I have found no evidence either here or in France—perhaps he thought of marriage.

What more logical? So—Rufus may have thought—Robert was married, and hoping to beget an heir? Well, two could play at that game. Why should he, Rufus, not provide his own heir, or at least try to? Union by marriage with some powerful family on the Continent would increase his influence, extend his dominions. Admittedly, it can hardly have been with the children of Duke William: married in 1094 to Philippa of Toulouse, he was to have two sons and five daughters, but not even the eldest daughter would have been nubile by 1100; at best there might be a prolonged betrothal, with cash down to guarantee the consummation. Elsewhere, however, there were a number of girls of suitable rank and marriageable age. Perhaps some day the evidence will come to light; at any rate, if such a likely project was envisaged and came to be known to Henry it would strike a deadly blow at the last of his hopes.

Even without it, 'Henry's fortunes,' says Barlow, 'were desperate.' Because, says Brooke, 'August 1100 might well seem his last real chance of securing the English throne.' And speed was essential, Poole points out, because Robert was drawing near; by early September, perhaps before the end of August, he would be back in the duchy. Now if ever was the time for ruthless action.

Three men and the crown of England: three brothers. Once before in living memory, Brooke recalls, three brothers in Spain had competed for power. One had been murdered, and one imprisoned for life by the third, who had seized all. No doubt that Henry had heard the story; for it seems to have been common knowledge at the Norman court that two of those same brothers had vied for the hand of one of the Conqueror's daughters, Agatha, who had died before the choice could be decided. Moreover, shortly before his death the Conqueror had received an offer of the crown of Galicia from rebels against the triumphantly surviving brother. Such memories offered a dangerous precedent to a man now thirty-three and verging on desperation.

Once again three brothers were aligned. The eldest, Robert, happy in his crusader's reputation, in his new-gained wealth, in his newly-wedded estate, sure of his eventual inheritance of the crown; the youngest, Henry, made cunning by years of frustration, ambitious, greedy, insecure; between them Rufus, the confident, powerful wearer of the crown, bestriding the narrow seas unchallenged. But what if the King should die?

VI

THE KING RIDES OUT

IN one account or another the chroniclers, principally Orderic Vitalis, William of Malmesbury and Geoffrey Gaimar, have a good deal to say about the last twenty-four hours of the King's life. And there is no reason why their statements of simple fact should not be taken seriously. What modern historians agree to reject is the long list of dreams, visions and portents, all wildly improbable—even Margaret Murray calls them 'childish'—and slanted to make the King appear so repulsive that his death by act of God becomes almost inescapable and certainly desirable. It is not the accuracy of the chroniclers which is in question; they are but passing on the legends approved by the Church. It may be wondered what would have happened had all the weird premonitions really been uttered ahead of the event, and had the King then lived to refute them; but those who guided the pens of the monkish chroniclers were on firm ground when they began to prophesy. The King was already dead and they knew it.

All the prophecies, however, were swallowed whole by Freeman, of whom Brooke says crisply : 'he never suppressed any of the evidence, however worthless.' Every fantastic vision, every improbable portent, all the wild rumours and unverifiable legends with which the events surrounding the King's death were deliberately obscured, he accepted without question. In the end, lost in the maze of superstition, he cried out plaintively : 'some kernel of truth there must surely be in so many tales of warning.' There is indeed; but not the kernel he was so determined to discover, the proof that a wicked man had been judged by God and that the judgment had been known beforehand.

Stripped of superstition the sequence of events seems straightforward enough. There are, it is true, some significant incidents, but they are not inexplicable and do not appear to weaken the evidence concerning the King's death; rather do they tend to strengthen it. A plot was hatching against his life; a plot that cannot have been contrived by one man alone. It may be that a warning was offered him and that he rejected it with a laugh; it would be like him if he did. It is said that in his later years he grew vain; say rather that he was pleased with himself, and not without reason. His was not the suspicious mind of some insecure and ever-anxious tyrant; his reign so far had been crowned with success; with ordinary luck and given the family longevity he could look forward to another twenty years of life, perhaps more. There was plenty of cash in the Treasury. Many exciting and profitable schemes were developing abroad. Surrounded by trusted friends, or so he thought, he had no cause to be anxious in the Forest.

Piecing together the chroniclers' accounts, and checking them when possible with the evidence of time and place, this is what seems to have happened. In the late afternoon of August 1st the King, returning from a day's hunting, dined at the *castel* with his friends. Nothing unusual is recorded about the meal, nor about how much he drank. His father had always been sparing of wine and there is no good reason for thinking that Rufus was less abstemious or some fault-finding chronicler would have said so. After dinner there may have been some minstrelsy or other entertainment. The Conqueror had had his '*joculator*', Henry was to have his 'mime'; and both these court comedians seem to have made a good thing out of their quips and antics, the first buying houses at Gloucester, the second land at Smithfield where he founded St Bartholomew's Priory. There is no record of any jester at the *castel*; maybe Rufus preferred to crack his own jokes. In any event he seems to have gone to bed at a normal hour.

In the middle of the night he woke up with a shout; called for the Chamberlain, who came running with other servants bearing lights. Perhaps it was a nightmare, as the chroniclers say, but it seems clear enough that he was taken ill. A stomach upset perhaps, some mild form of food-poisoning or too much venison for dinner; the only remarkable thing is that no one else in his entourage seems to have suffered in the same way. No record hints at foul play, yet if the King's cupbearer at the *castel* was that same Eudo *dapifer* who had married the elder of the two Clare girls (Rohese, sister of Alice Tirel of Poix) and was known to be a close friend of Henry's, one might be tempted to think that he had doctored the wine, perhaps so as to render the King less active on the following day; but for this there is not the slightest documentary evidence.[1] If any suspicions were voiced by the King, the facts were suppressed by the chroniclers who then sub-stituted, as the cause of the indisposition, the horrendous vision of torrents of blood and blasphemy culminating in the death of the dreamer—a nightmare so implausible that, given its posthu-mous telling when it could no longer be contradicted by the King, one can only suppose it to have been a part of the propa-ganda campaign against him.

The King sat up for most of the night and, in the morning, stayed in bed much longer than usual. When at length he did get up he still felt so shaky that he remained indoors; hunting was out of the question. At some time during the morning Robert fitz-Hamon came to report that a monk was waiting below, anxious to relate a warning dream. Perhaps the man really had a warning to convey and chose to wrap it up in a vision that would neither warn the plotters nor compromise him personally. But Rufus was in no mood to receive him. 'Just like a monk!' he is said to have grumbled. 'He's dreaming for money. Tell him to go away—and given him a hundred shillings.' If the reaction seems natural, the amount hardly endorses the view generally expressed by the chroniclers of the King's niggardliness to all ecclesiastics.

Towards midday the King felt well enough to discuss some 'serious business', though its nature is not revealed; and in the afternoon he is said to have had a long conversation with the Lord

---

[1] See Appendix F in Douglas, *William the Conqueror*. 'On poisoning as a method of political action in the 11th century.' Both William of Malmes-bury and Orderic Vitalis mention the possibility of such action elsewhere, but not in the case of Rufus.

of Poix, Walter Tirel, on foreign affairs, some part of which was apparently overheard since it was later reported, and embellished, by Geoffrey Gaimar. Here, however, one must again be careful. When the chroniclers quote long informal conversations in what purport to be the actual words used they are only following the method then frequently employed to give verisimilitude to what they thought had most probably been said. From these passages of direct speech one cannot expect the same detailed accuracy as in the recording of simple facts; reliable eavesdroppers were not always at hand to take the speeches down verbatim. The King, moreover, spoke Norman French which was not invariably the mother-tongue of the clerics at court, and the chroniclers then put his words into Latin, the translation lending itself to distortion. True, Gaimar wrote in French, but he used a rhymed verse-form into which there crept, almost inevitably with poetic licence, a good deal of fiction.

The caution need not, however, be applied too rigorously to brief comments or chance remarks spoken openly. They would be heard by, very probably, numerous witnesses standing near, would be repeated, discussed, remembered, and eventually written down by some clerk at court. This seems to have been what happened at the end of the King's conversation with Tirel; the last sentences were overheard as they rejoined their friends. There is no reason to disbelieve the words quoted, but they have sometimes been given undue importance. Margaret Murray—whose theories, says Brooke after a careful analysis, 'can be dismissed as fantasy' (and he is not alone in his condemnation)—goes so far as to suggest that Rufus was asking Tirel to shoot him dead in the name of some abstruse, and in any case anachronistic, witchcraft ritual; a request, it is hardly necessary to add, entirely out of keeping with every-thing known of the King's buoyant spirits and extrovert character.

In plain language all the King said was: 'Remember what you've heard, Walter, and take appropriate action.' To which Tirel replied: 'So I will, my lord.' Nothing more than that. If Gaimar is right in saying that affairs on the continent had just been discussed, it is conceivable that the 'action' referred to con-

cerned Poitou and the Duke of Aquitaine. But further specula-
tion seems unjustified.[1]

Some time after this conversation the King decided to dine
with his guests in the hall. The exact hour at which the meal
began is not known; the chroniclers give little help and few since
their day seem to have sought an answer to the question, although
it has some bearing upon the timing of later events; and timing
becomes of ever greater importance as the drama unfolds. Freeman says that the King dined at 'the early hour usual in those
days', and to the conventional mid-19th century gentleman anything before seven might seem early. Probably, for Rufus, the
hour for dinner was when he said so. But considering what had
gone before, and looking ahead to the events that followed, I
make it roughly four o'clock, which seems to fit the few known
facts. At that time the King was apparently in good health again;
and having, presumably, fasted all day, he must have developed
a healthy appetite, for it was noted that he ate and drank more
than was his custom. (Is this perhaps a hint that he was fuddled,
or at least less sharply perceptive than usual?) One may therefore suppose a fairly long function, lasting perhaps until five.
Afterwards he would want to stretch his legs, perhaps retire to
his chamber; take a stroll outside, a glance at the weather; discuss hunting prospects. At about this time one or two of his companions—among them Robert fitz-Hamon—apparently advised
him, in view of his recent indisposition and of the lateness of the
hour, to give up hunting that day. Others are represented by
Gaimar as waiting impatiently in the courtyard below, anxious
to get moving after a day's idleness, chaffing the King for his indecision. This may have been at some time after half-past five,
and it seems to have been close on six when the King at length
decided to hunt.

---

[1] The Duke was certainly in a hurry to complete the negotiations and get
the money. Later that year, when the death of Rufus had dashed his hopes
of a quick settlement, he turned to Bertrand de Saint-Gilles and ceded to
him—for an undisclosed sum—the County of Toulouse which, in his wife's
name, he had annexed only two years previously. See Richard: *Histoire des
Comtes de Poitou.*

By that hour he would have consulted his Chief Hunter to find out what arrangements had been made and which woods could most usefully be hunted so late in the day. In the ordinary course of events at the *castel* provisional arrangements would be put to the King on the previous evening, and once his preference for some particular district was known—depending on conditions of weather and the number of deer reported—messengers would be sent out to warn the local keeper of the Walk to stand by. An early-morning start would then be usual, so as to cover the distance, get in a day's hunting, and return to dine and sleep at the *castel*, since no other lodge could accommodate so numerous a party.

On this occasion, however, with the King indisposed, alternatives were doubtless progressively curtailed until, by six o'clock, it became evident that only in the nearest Walk would there be any real chance of sport within the two remaining hours of useful daylight. It therefore seems likely that when, at the King's bidding, the Chief Hunter summoned the keeper of the Walk to give an opinion, he advised beating the dense woods towards Canterton manor and less than a mile to the east of the *castel*. Huntsmen and hounds could be at their posts within half an hour; the weather was fine, the prospects for several kills before sundown would seem good.

The King then dressed for hunting. What he wore may appear to be of small importance; for so short an expedition on a warm summer's evening both clothing and equipment would have been light. It seems likely that he pulled on one of those plain tunics shown in the Bayeux tapestry, russet-brown or neutral olive-green, low-collared, belted at the waist and reaching down to mid-thigh. Below this he may well have worn the narrow jodhpur-like *heuse*, perhaps of buckskin, with soft leather boots laced with deerskin thongs about the ankles. It was while an attendant was lacing the boots that there occurred the incident of the arrows. A man said to be an armourer, possibly the fletcher, came up to offer some newly-made shafts, reported to be six in number. The King, accepting them, turned to give a couple to Walter Tirel, remarking : 'The best arrows for the best shot.' Some have found in this incident, too, a portent of doom; but all the words seem to show —and they have the ring of truth—is that, although Tirel was 'a stranger at court', his marksmanship was already well-known; possibly it had been proved during the preceding two or three days of hunting.

It must have been nearly half-past six when the King came out of the *castel* to the courtyard where the horses were waiting and where, according to Gaimar, his friends greeted him with laughing comments expressing their delight to be off at last. The King then mounted and led the way down the inclosure; but before reaching the entrance gate (on the west side?) he was stopped by the announcement, made perhaps by the guard on duty, that another monk had arrived, this time with an urgent letter from Serlo, the Norman Abbot of St Peter's at Gloucester. There seem to have been an unusual number of monks about in the Forest that day—in the muddled legends of a later date the number is stepped up to include a wandering bishop—but the evidence concerning this particular monk seems too detailed to be disregarded.

The letter—read out perhaps by a court cleric, perhaps by the monk himself, since the King and all those present in the hunting party were illiterate—said that yet another monk, at Serlo's abbey, had just had another dream, a complicated vision of Christ and the Virgin Mary, whose underlying purpose was to warn the King against hunting that day. Here again a genuine warning may have been intended. Some whisper of a conspiracy may have reached Gloucester, loud enough to alarm the loyal abbot. But again the King would have none of it. Dismissing the monk, he urged his horse forward. 'Does Serlo think,' he exclaimed impatiently, 'that I believe in the dreams of every snoring monk?' And laughing he uttered his last recorded jest : 'Does he take me for an Englishman—to put my trust in any old wives' tale?'

And so he rode out. In good spirits; keen to hunt; the bluff, unquestioned master, surrounded by friends and servants; fearing no man. In half an hour he would be dead.

VII

THE HUNT AND THE HUNTERS

WITH the King and his friends on horseback heading away from the inclosure, there is time to consider their actions before they arrive at the hunting ground in the woods towards Canterton. We know whence they came, and we know where the King went. But what of the others? By what route did they approach the hollow? In what manner did they all, the King included, intend to hunt?

About the hunting there are several important points to be cleared up, since they have a direct bearing upon the mystery of the King's death. First in order of importance, it is abundantly plain from three independent sources—William of Malmesbury, Orderic Vitalis, and Geoffrey Gaimar—that this was no deer hunt of the sort to which, with a large pack of hounds and mounted huntsmen, we are accustomed today whether in the New Forest or in the forests of France. Here the hunters were on foot and the deer were driven to them.

For this sort of hunting there are, obviously, a few simple but essential requisites. First, and most obvious, the hunters must stand downwind of the quarry. Then there must be a thicket in which the deer are known to be lying, and an open space to which they can be driven by beaters working from upwind. Facing this open space there must be another wood, on the fringe of which the hunters must be able to stand concealed but with an unobstructed line of sight. In the days before firearms a further condition was imposed by the weapon used, since the range at which a hunter drawing the long-bow could be reasonably sure of hitting a moving target so as to inflict a swiftly mortal wound would be no more that about fifty yards; and the most suitable width of the glade

62

between the two woods would therefore be about equal to this. On the other hand, too narrow a glade—a track or bridle-path, for instance—would allow the stag to be seen for too short a time and at too awkward an angle for a well-aimed and effective shot.

From the Rufus Stone it can be seen how exactly the locality complies both with the requirements of the hunt and with the details of what is said to have happened at the time of the King's death. An open space and a glade lie to the west, with woods on either hand each within the fifty-yard range. And from this setting something of value can at once be deduced. William of Malmesbury says that the King, watching his wounded stag, was facing into the sunset: that stag, before turning on being hit, can only have come from one of the two woods to the west. Since it must have been advancing downwind, in the evening of August 2nd the wind must have been blowing from the westerly quarter and probably, in the light of circumstances to be considered later, from the north-west. Its strength is unlikely to have been great, since a stiff breeze would have made accurate shooting difficult, in which case the King would probably have cancelled the already delayed hunt. It can therefore be said that, towards sundown of a fine summer's evening, the wind was light, perhaps not so much as five miles an hour at ground level. It may, nevertheless, have exerted some small influence upon the shooting.

For the time being I was more concerned to discover where, with Rufus taking his stand at the site of the Stone and Tirel not too far away, the remaining seven men of the party had gone. And, whatever the probabilities, it is impossible to be certain on this point, though fortunately it matters very little. Provided that reasonable account is taken of time, distance, woodland topography and wind-direction, the shooting-line can be conjectured with sufficient accuracy.

I began my calculations from the summit of the knoll, that useful observation-post some fifty yards to the east of the Rufus Stone.

When the party set out it must have consisted of at least a dozen horsemen in all and probably as many attendants and hunt servants on foot. It is likely that there was in addition a small mounted detachment of armed men for the normal duty of guarding the King and also to take charge of the horses when the hunters dismounted. After leaving the *castel* inclosure the party would follow the short track between the trees down to the ancient road, which they would then follow westward towards the Stoney Cross plain. After covering some two to three hundred yards a brief halt may have been called to allow a first group to peel off to the right along a track leading in the general direction of Canterton manor. Another couple of hundred yards farther on a second group may similarly have turned aside, to take a path running in roughly the same direction; leaving the King and Walter Tirel, with their attendants, to ride the short distance remaining to the point where a bridle-path—roughly the modern road—led down into the hollow. This supposition agrees with Orderic's statement that 'the hunters were scattered in their various positions', and with William of Malmesbury's: 'the party split up in the woods and the King was left alone with Tirel.' But it is impossible to say exactly how the seven men were grouped or in what order they proceeded.

It can be taken as certain that all dismounted and left their horses to be held either upon the road or in the woods a short distance from it. Otherwise, although the whole party must at all times have been well downwind of the intended quarry, the trampling of horses and the jingle of harness echoing through the evening stillness of the woods must have given clear warning to the deer ahead. Thus the better part of a quarter of a mile is likely to have been covered on foot and with increasing caution as the guides led the way to the previously selected stands. There is no special reason for thinking that each of the seven stood alone with his guide and personal attendant; they may have stood in pairs, each pair separated from the next by a safe interval of intervening trees, of say fifty yards. Under these conditions the shooting line might extend from a short distance beyond the knoll for something like a hundred and fifty yards to the north-east.

To get some idea whether this imagined line was likely or even possible, I left the knoll and walked eastward into the woods. Here it soon became clear that to establish anything with the least degree of certainty is out of the question. Changes have been imposed that make of the woods a palimpsest through which it is next to impossible to decipher the original document. Gleaning scraps of information, I walked on.

The ground falls away fairly sharply beyond the knoll and what must once have been a broad ride leads approximately north-east. Well-marked but confusing tracks branch off through the woods to spaces where, in relatively recent times, there has been some felling of timber; but upon the ride itself a number of fine trees, beeches especially, have sprung up and grown to a girth and a height which they cannot have attained in less than several centuries, thus proving the ride's antiquity. The denser woods bordering it to the south are also of great age and they present an irregular but distinguishable line, along which the Norman hunters may have taken their stands so as to shoot, across the then unobstructed ride, at deer driven from the thicket to the north.

But although this theoretical positioning was not impossible, it was all discouragingly vague. To seek a likely alternative I turned sharply aside, noting that owing to the fall of the ground east of the knoll the Rufus Stone was lost to sight; no one could have shot the King from this side. I now thrust into the thicket to the north of the ride. Here too, the impression is of age: undergrowth that has never been thinned, overcrowded trees, decay and natural regeneration, all point to it, and, though most of the trees are far from handsome, there are oaks among them of certainly no more than second or third generation from the time of the Conquest. On a compass course, north-west, I made my way diagonally through until, roughly seventy yards on, I came to the wood's abrupt verge and faced, across a gravelly tree-dotted 'lawn', what is known today as Upper Canterton.

The style is far too grand for so small a locality, consisting of little more than an old thatched cottage and a modern inn—a pleasant place ineptly named the 'Sir Walter Tyrrell'—but it

E

does serve as a useful landmark whose position has not changed across the centuries. According to the Domesday record, quoted by Wise, one Chenna held Canterton manor of Edward the Confessor and still held it, early in 1087, of William the Conqueror. Although the original holding had been slightly reduced by the afforestation decree of 1079, the reduction does not appear to have affected the southern boundary which remains largely unaltered to this day. Since forest law forbade any inclosing of the land or interference with the game one may assume that, in August 1100, Chenna (or his heir) would be only too glad to have the King's men drive the mischievous deer from his few fertile acres. With the ancient boundary still in existence, and allowing for a few natural changes, I found it easy to imagine a drive from the Canterton land, across the open, towards the margin of the wood I had just traversed.

I now had two conjectural but possible lines, of which the second was perhaps the more probable. Sketching both lines into my map I could see that they lay at about the right distance from the *castel* at Malwood—in view of the shortness of time available for the hunters to move into position—and also that the left-hand (most westerly) man of either line would stand at a sufficient distance from the King (at the Stone) for the chroniclers to report truthfully that Rufus and Tirel were 'alone', meaning away from the party of seven. With the lines running more or less parallel and facing, by compass, between west-north-west and north-north-west, one may gain some slight confirmation that the wind that evening blew from the north-west.

Useless to venture any further. To the east no more could be discovered. Leaving the seven hunters on their most probable shooting-line where, Orderic says, they 'established themselves in the wood and waited eagerly for the prey, with weapons ready', I made my way back through the trees and across the road to the Rufus Stone.

All this of course supposes what must certainly have been the case, that the hunt was carefully organized. Too often it is said that the hunting of Norman times was nothing but the King's 'cruel sport' indulged in for his 'selfish pleasure', and the impression is given that whenever they had nothing better to do the bad 'Red King' and his dissolute friends wandered boozily into the Forest to maim or to slaughter every miserable beast they could find. No doubt there was, then as now, some wild and primitive pleasure to be derived from the chase, from stalking, from skilfully hitting a moving target, from proudly returning with trophies of the hunt; but there was a far more serious purpose to it than that. First and foremost was the getting of meat for the King's table; and not only for the King himself but, as Poole points out, for the whole of the royal court, perhaps six or seven hundred strong. Compared to stringy beef and tough old mutton, a well-hung haunch of venison was a delicacy more favoured then than now. The skins too had more widespread uses: for mats, hangings and bed-coverings, for deerskin jackets and buckskin breeches, for soft *heuse* and ankle-boots, and thongs for the countless purposes of tying and binding. Even the antlers retained their ancient value as primitive picks and shovels and also, as to this day, as hafts for knives. 'Sport' apart, hunting was good business in the affairs of the King.

Allowing for the known circumstance that the deer were to be driven to a line of dismounted hunters, the manner in which the hunt was conducted in the evening of August 2nd is fairly easy to follow. Back at the *castel*, once the King had decided to hunt, it would be for the Chief Hunter to get things going with the help of the keeper of the Walk. This Chief Hunter seems unlikely to have had control of all hunting in the King's realm, but rather of New Forest hunting only; certainly, whatever the scope of his appointment, a royal nominee in constant attendance upon the King in the hunting-court, he was one of the knightly class of Norman origin. The keeper of the Walk, on the other hand, his men and hunt servants, must all have been foresters born and bred, quiet West Saxons, wholly uneducated by modern standards but surpassingly wise concerning the ways of the deer in woodlands whose every tree was familiar to them. Thirty-four years after Hastings, twenty-one since the afforestation decree, a new generation had come to manhood in the Forest, one that knew nothing of battle or local rebellion, that accepted Norman rule without question and, if only the more promptly to obey orders, had acquired a useful smattering of the Norman tongue. The King and his friends, for all their scorn of the stolidly superstitious *engles* and the harsh-sounding Anglo-Saxon speech, did not spurn the foresters' expert knowledge of the chase and may even, were the hunting good, have felt for them a measure of contemptuous liking. They had certainly nothing to fear from them, least of all the King.

As soon as he had received his orders from the Chief Hunter, the keeper of the Walk would send out to alert those of his men who were, presumably, already waiting on the far side of the woods where the deer were known to be lying. A line, or rather a crescent, would then be formed of men who, for the sake of clarity, may be called 'beaters', whatever local name may then have been used. Given the shortness of time before dusk, it can be assumed that only two woods, east and west of the bridle-path, were to be beaten that evening, that about a dozen men would be required for each and that, additionally, there would be several huntsmen in each group leading 'tufter'-hounds[1] to find and select grown stags or fat young bucks and to let be the does, at this season in milk and still suckling their fawns. Having taken position, well upwind in the chosen woods, the lines of beaters would then wait in silence for the hunting party to arrive and for the keeper's signal to close in.

The keeper, meanwhile, would already have allotted to each noble hunter, or pair of hunters, the forester necessary to guide him through the woods. That this was done seems certain; because even supposing every member of the party to have hunted in this part of the Forest before, which is far from sure, none of them would be able to find exactly the stand now selected for him by, one may suppose, the keeper on the orders of the Chief

---

[1] From *touffeteur*: a hound trained to work in the clumps (*touffes*) or thickets (*bois touffus*).

Hunter. Had they gone alone they would either have strayed in the dense woods and have missed the hunting altogether or, blundering on too far, have scared away the deer. Walter Tirel in particular; a stranger at court, there is nothing to show that he had ever been in the New Forest before, and he could not have found his stand unaided. And until the proposed shooting-line was fully manned there could be no driving forward the deer.

Probably none of these forest guides, however expert in all that concerned the woods and the habits of deer, would also be able to act as 'bearers' or 'loaders', since such humble subordinates—some of them may well have been boys—were not commonly trained to the bow. But in any event each of the hunters must, in addition to his guide, have been accompanied by his own personal attendant—'li archer' according to Gaimar—to carry spare arrows, a spare bowstring, perhaps a spare bow, to 'mark' the quarry and to note the effect of the hunter's shot. Certainly the King would have such a man with him, and it is highly improbable that any of his friends, 'great men' accustomed to command personal service at all times, would go hunting unattended. Two men (but one at least) to each hunter appears to have been normal, and the point—which, it will be seen later, is of some importance—seems to be proved by internal evidence in the chroniclers' accounts.

Once the detailed arrangements had been made at the *castel*, the keeper of the Walk, leaving the Chief Hunter to accompany the King, would ride on ahead of the party. He had a job to do and a longer journey to make than the rest: a circuitous route taking him, first, a good half-mile along the Stoney Cross road; then, bearing right, down into the furzy hollow over towards the edge of Fritham Plain; and so, bearing right again, to the upwind flank of the woods to be beaten. Here he would take his stand, in all probability at the south-west corner of the most westerly wood. From this point—I am jumping ahead here, for I had not yet inspected it—he would be in touch with the nearest of the beaters and he would also have a clear view of the grove of trees, some one hundred and twenty yards to the east, on the fringe of which the King was to take his stand. The moment the King arrived there, the Chief Hunter at his side would announce the fact—doubtless by hand signal so as not to break silence and alarm the deer—and the keeper would then pass the word to the beaters to start closing in. Some five minutes later the first of the deer could be expected to break cover in the direction of the King. (One may leave out of account the probably similar but independent arrangements made for the seven hunters to the east, since they have no direct bearing upon those made for the King and Tirel to the west.)

It will be recalled that, by careful reckoning, it was approximately half-past six when the hunting party rode out of the *castel* inclosure. It would take them, riding and then walking, between fifteen and twenty minutes in all to reach their respective stands in the shooting line. As nearly as can be estimated therefore it was about ten minutes to seven when the King, led by the Chief Hunter and accompanied by his archer-attendant, came to the position now marked by the Rufus Stone.

It must be stressed that none of the foregoing is as conjectural as it may appear. Theory has been made to conform strictly to the facts recorded by the chroniclers, to the topography of the woods, and to the conditions of hunting. A further point to be considered is scarcely conjectural at all. It concerns the carrying of the bow.

Under the Normans very few of the small number of native Saxon inhabitants of the New Forest ever openly carried a bow; even to own one was dangerously unwise, since, with the shooting of all manner of game prohibited under forest law, it would be as much as a man's eyes were worth to be caught with a weapon of the chase. Did his neighbour but bear him a grudge, how easy to arouse suspicion by pointing to the remains of some game-animal placed with malice near the victim's cottage. If there were then to be found by the Regarders, the guardians of forest law, the damning evidence of so much as a bowstring, the suspect would be dragged off to the Court of Attachment, passed on to the

Court of Swainmote, and remanded in custody to the Justice-in-Eyre who came round only once in three years, if then. It would be a lucky man indeed who, once arrested, survived to see his home again.

To this rule there were hardly any exceptions. The paramount duty of New Forest dwellers being to preserve both 'vert and venaison' for the King and never to hunt, few would need to carry more than a staff and, perhaps, a knife. Only a small number of those patrolling the Forest, chief among them the keepers of the Walks, would normally carry the bow, and would indeed be required to carry it so as to put down deer maimed by shooting, injured by chance, or sick; and this not out of humane consideration, but in order to maintain the health and fitness of the herds as a whole. It may also have been a keeper's duty to kill deer wounded during a hunt, though probably, once the King and his friends had shown their skill and had their sport, it would be the privilege of the Norman knight-huntsmen—who were, of course, entitled to carry the bow at all times—to give the *coup-de-grâce* to any wounded deer escaping from the shooting-line. For the same purpose, the bringing down of escaping deer, hounds were probably held at either end of the shooting-line; but the men holding these hounds, and presumably letting them slip only at the command of the Chief Hunter, a knight-huntsman or the keeper of the Walk, would have no need of a bow.

From these various considerations it appears certain that, with the keeper of the Walk and his men at a distance and busy driving the deer from the chosen wood, no Saxon bowman stood within effective bowshot of the King in the evening of August 2nd. It is also apparent that, of the very few men, perhaps five in all including attendants and forest guides, standing within range of the King at the hour when the hunt began, only Walter Tirel and the Chief Hunter were equipped with the long-bow. As a knight-huntsman of rank, the Chief Hunter was of necessity an expert archer. So, it seems, was Tirel.

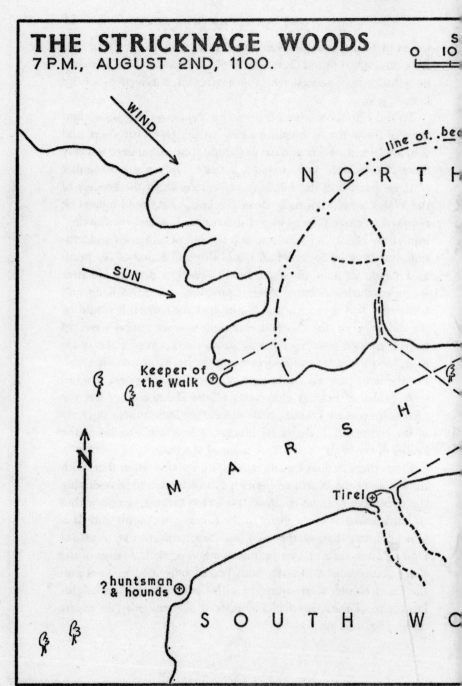

THE STRICKNAGE WOODS
7 P.M., AUGUST 2ND, 1100.

WIND

SUN

line of... bec

N O R T H

Keeper of
the Walk

M A R S H

N

Tirel

? huntsman
& hounds

S O U T H W O

0   10   S

Sketch map only. See page 84 for explanation.

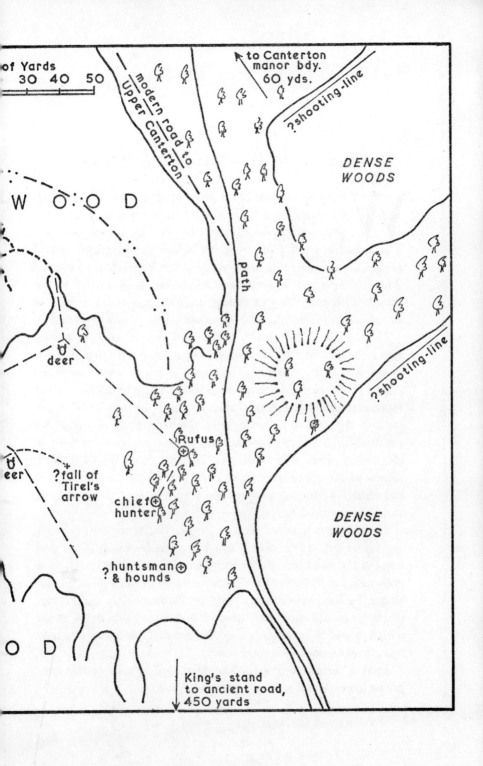

of Yards
30 40 50

to Canterton manor bdy. 60 yds.

modern road to Upper Canterton

?shooting-line

DENSE WOODS

W O O D

path

deer

?shooting-line

Rufus

?fall of Tirel's arrow

deer

chief hunter

DENSE WOODS

?huntsman & hounds

O D

King's stand to ancient road, 450 yards

VIII

THE WOOD AND THE TREES

WHEN I returned to the Stone from my tour of the woods towards Upper Canterton it was nearly quarter to seven, Summer Time, of course; by the sun, a quarter to six. There was a good hour to spare before the imagined arrival of the King when, this being August 9th, equivalent to August 2nd 1100, the conditions of light would be almost exactly reproduced. This gave me just enough time to explore the fringes of the woods to the west and to take some initial measurements.

Here again, in the need to explore and to measure, the personal narrative is hardly to be avoided, there being no other detailed description of the neighbourhood upon which to draw. Nor is the scale of the available maps sufficiently large to allow a clear representation of the stands taken by the King and Tirel, of the path of the deer and the flight of the arrows, all of which are essential to an understanding of the events recorded by the chroniclers. Even the Ordnance Survey's National Grid plan, drawn to the generous scale of twenty-five inches to the mile, is too restricted; for my purpose something at least twice as large would be required.

Not that the National Grid and other Ordnance Survey maps are unhelpful. They have yielded invaluable information, and some of the older editions have enabled me to re-discover features obliterated in course of time by new roads or buildings or, for instance, by the now-disused airfield on Fritham Plain. And it can of course be assumed that these scientifically-drawn maps attain a high degree of accuracy, so high indeed that it is hard to see how any error can possibly have occurred.

That a certain local error has developed in spite of this cannot be blamed on the cartographers of today.

The initial error occurred more than a century ago and I should never have learned of it without the help of the Forestry Commission at Lyndhurst. It has to do with the positioning of a woodland place-name and, since the Ordnance Survey never publish any name on a map without the written authority of the owners of the land, in this case the Crown, any serious inaccuracy must be due in the first place to faulty information supplied in the past to the Deputy Surveyor of the New Forest. Or rather, given the increasing magnitude of the error, to successive Deputy Surveyors holding office from the end of the 18th century to the second half of the 19th. How their advisers came to countenance the mistake and then to repeat it is a mystery; perhaps they were careless; certainly they failed to consult those men of the Malwood Walk who knew every wood by name and knew that every name had its own significance.

The woodland area in question has been known since time immemorial as the Stricknage, though from what has happened to it on paper over the past hundred years it might almost better be termed the Shrinkage. Even more remarkable is the fact, for which I am indebted to the Forestry Commission, that it has not only shrunk, it has shifted position.

On the first official map of the New Forest ever made, published in 1789 and known as Driver's Map, the Stricknage Wood is given an acreage of one hundred and fifty and the pinpoint centre of the name is placed 540 metres to the west of the Rufus Stone. On the Ordnance Survey map of 1871 the acreage has been reduced to forty, whilst the centre of the name has moved to 592 metres west of the Rufus Stone. On the latest National Grid (1 : 2500) Plan, revised in 1960, the acreage is down to thirty-five and the centre-point is now 626 metres west of the Rufus Stone; a total westward shift of 86 metres. Did Birnam Wood thus come to Dunsinane?

It is not the acreage that matters; in fact it cannot be measured accurately at all, because the extent of the wood was never clearly defined by the men of the Walk who alone can have known it. What does matter—if only to the inquiring historian—is the wood's position prior to its strange and apparently motiveless journeying to the west. Driver's Map of 1789 fortunately supplies the answer to this, giving the eastern boundary of the Stricknage Wood as the track leading south from Upper Canterton towards Castle Malwood. Originally, therefore, the wood embraced the area of lawn, heath and trees lying immediately to the west of the Rufus Stone, including the Stone itself and the grove about it. In the absence of defined limits Driver's extension to the west seems natural enough, since there are no other place-names until one comes, south of west, to Fritham Plain or, due west, to the Long Beech inclosure. But the old, eastern boundary should never have been omitted from the later maps.

Once that well-marked boundary has been replaced, the name Stricknage is seen to be one of the most significant of pointers. It is not, as might be thought from the spelling 'Strickenage' given by J. R. Wise, intended to mark a wood so old as justifiably to be termed 'stricken with age'. Here the word is a noun whose origin may well date from the mid-12th century when the ancient speech was merging into Middle English. A noun formed by linking the Anglo-Saxon *strican* (to strike) to the common French suffix *-age* denoting 'place where'. Perhaps it was a keeper of the Walk or, conceivably, the tenant of Canterton manor, who first designated the hollow where Rufus had been stricken down the Wood of the Stricknage. Today, despite its misplacing, the name endures to identify the locality where the Stone pinpoints the site.

The wood lies beyond the open 'lawn' to the west of the Stone. To take it all in at one glance is next to impossible; the scene is too broad and its most obvious feature, a long natural glade of an average width of some forty yards, splits it down the middle to make two similar but apparently separate woods. And as two woods I decided to treat it, naming the wood to my right North Stricknage, the one to my left South Stricknage. I did this for convenience and clarity, and not because of any evidence that the woods were at any time so named by native foresters.

Using the compass to take bearings upon the salient points of each, I set out almost due west but inclining a little to the left so as to reach the South wood first. An unpleasant walk, for the recent rains had not yet drained from the slippery clay underlying the thin grass of the 'lawn', and the farther I went the worse it became as the increasingly rough ground sloping gently up towards the west was broken by tussocks of coarser grass alternating with tufts of wiry heather, interspersed with patches of deep mud. Upon one such, a tussock broader than the rest and forming with its accompaniment of spindly rushes something resembling a large molehill, solid in appearance, I set my foot down confidently; and went through into a swamp-hole of oily water and slimy clay that came well over my ankles—a minor *contretemps* that served its purpose by reminding me of two quoted passages in my notebook.

The first is from Cornish. Writing, it will be remembered, more than seventy years before my visit, he described the land to the west of the Rufus Stone as a 'marshy slope', to which he added : 'wood does not grow on it now, and never could have grown, for the nature of the soil has not changed, and remains in the same condition for the growth or non-growth of timber as in the days of the Conquest.' The second comes from nearly eight centuries earlier. Geoffrey Gaimar, describing the events of August 2nd, says that the King and Walter Tirel were hunting 'in a densely wooded part of the Forest near a marsh.' There could be no doubt of the marsh; it lay at my feet, and to either side stood the dense woods.

In passing it is worth noting that, although during a dry summer the swamp patches in the glade are few and small, after a season of heavy rains the whole area tends to become marshy and so further to justify Gaimar's description. In Norman times the hollow may well have been marshier throughout the year, since the various shallow gutters, some cut across the 'lawn', others scraped on the far side of the North wood and draining towards Upper Canterton, are all of much more recent origin; and the gradient of the slope in the main glade can never have been sufficient, by itself, to carry off the normal rainfall.

On reaching the corner of the South wood I halted, facing west. Seen in profile the front is nearly but not altogether straight; there are small bays and capes, with here and there a tree standing out from the rest, so that I had the impression of a rank of ill-dressed troops. And pursuing the analogy it occurred to me that had it been possible to take, intermittently over the centuries, a series of film-shots and then to show them in a single projection there would have been visible a slight, continual fluctuation as the line of trees strove to 'pick up the dressing'. Only a small movement, no more than a few feet either way; because if, within the wood, the loam is deep enough to ensure with the help of a mild, damp climate the perennial renewal of packed vegetation, outside it, drawing an unalterable line beyond which no tree can take root, lies the great mass of gravel. A mass that has lain upon the whole New Forest area, say the geologists, ever since the sea receded from it some forty thousand years ago.[1]

Some changes in outward appearance occur, of course, with the seasons and through the various combinations of hard or mild winters with dry or rainy summers, but they are not enough to alter the general configuration of the wood. Here, in fact, I had found two things which all those with expert knowledge of the Forest, from Wise to Edlin, had led me to expect. First, a wood of unquestionable antiquity, whose tendency to outward advance is halted at the limit of fertile soil. Secondly, a natural glade unchanging in its inability to produce timber: 'a poor acid soil deficient in phosphates', as the Forestry Commission report puts it. On the thin surface-layer of clay little more than coarse grass can grow between the tussocks of sorry heather and the scanty rushes that spring up about the frequent patches of marsh. Ponies, deer and cattle may browse upon the green fringes of the wood; there is little sustenance for them in the glade whose soil no race of men has ever turned. 'Larks' lees' the older foresters call this sort of land that is not, and never was, worth the trouble of tilling. For the purpose of my inquiry, however, the glade and its woods

---

[1] See 'The Geological Structure of the New Forest' by L. E. Tavener in the *Forestry Commission's Guide*, 1961.

offered a single quality of inestimable value: that of immutability, a quality noted as one of the outstanding features of the Forest by all the leading authorities.

Walking west along the fringe of the South wood I could see at my feet clear evidence of the ceaseless battle waged on the frontier. From the foremost trees the seed is scattered outward, some of it falling beyond the wood's natural boundary. There, in a sprinkling of top-soil amid the pebbles, it finds enough nourishment to enable it to sprout. The seedlings spring up bravely between the tufts of grass, rise to a height of three or four inches upon the new, false margin, and then perish, for they can strike no roots. Of those that survive the nibbling of ponies, of the deer that still roam these woods when the tourists have gone, almost all wither before the return of spring. The clay and the gravel reassert their authority; the old margin remains static.

About twenty yards along the front I came upon the entrance to a miniature glade leading south. Not much more than six feet wide at its mouth, it broadens slightly within and winds back for perhaps half a dozen yards before tapering off where the trees hem it in. One small channel, presumably an ancient deer-path, leads on through the wood; but no man-made marks are anywhere visible, no thinning or felling, so that one may suppose the glade to be a natural formation that has stood unaltered for ages.

On the western side of this narrow inlet a rounded clump juts very slightly forward into the main glade. Though none of its few trees is of great antiquity, the soil conditions appear to indicate that within it timber has always flourished. The clump is less than ten yards across and beyond it, to the west, the outline curves sharply back to merge with dense brushwood linking it to the true face of the South wood. From the back of the notch thus formed between the clump and the wood proper a well-marked deer-path runs in to wind uphill, south by east, whilst towards the front of it there is sufficient loam to support a few dwarf hollies, gorse, and some tufts of rather healthier looking heather than can be found in the open. In fairly distant times a small tree, possibly a thorn, also stood here and then perished, for a broken and long withered limb is just discernible above dead roots lying hidden amid rank grass. From these and other signs it seems evident that, whatever grew or did not grow here in the remote past, an indentation of sorts, linked to the deer-path, has shaped the wood at this point for almost as long as the wood itself has existed. And facing about to look back, past the trees in the clump and across the broad open space of the main glade to a corresponding indentation in the leafy margin forty yards away, it struck me forcibly that here, concealed in the notch, a hunter would find the ideal stand in which to wait for deer breaking cover from the North wood.

Turning away, I covered another fifty yards or so to the west and reached a point where the wood bends back at right-angles, runs south for some half a dozen yards, then makes another right-angle bend to the west again before finally curving away to the south. This marks the end of the wood upon the western side, beyond which I had no need to explore. The nick formed by the two sharp bends at the wood's corner bears all the usual signs of age; old trees crowd haphazardly about it and the thicket within is black as night. Brushwood has spread over the floor of the nick, proving the presence of some good top-soil; perhaps a tree stood here and fell, or was felled, in remote times. But a sharp corner there must always have been; a convenient spot at which to station a huntsman just out of sight of the main glade. A huntsman with, perhaps, a couple of hounds.

I only mention this small point because, among later chroniclers, one Peter Blois (quoted by J. R. Wise) contributes a vivid detail that may concern it.[1] At the time of the King's death, he says, 'hounds were hunting a stag up a hill'. Little notice has been taken of this, naturally enough; but it may well describe exactly what happened. The stag at which the King had shot 'fled westward', up the long slope of the glade. A huntsman with a couple

[1] This incident is mentioned in Gales's *Rerum Anglicarum Scriptores*, published Oxford, 1684.

of hounds posted at the western corner of the South wood could not fail to see it pass and see that it was wounded. It would then be his duty, perhaps at the command of the keeper of the Walk across the glade, to let slip the hounds so as to bring the beast down before it reached the cover of scrub and trees on the rise bordering Fritham Plain half a mile to the west. A small point indeed; and yet, to the picture formed from Gaimar's dense woods about a marsh, from William of Malmesbury's wounded stag fleeing into the sunset towards Leland's Fritham, Peter Blois's hounds running uphill seem to add a credible detail.

Crossing the glade towards the western edge of the North wood I found the going, over countless heathery tussocks each surrounded by its own channel of mud, even rougher than before. The wood itself has a much more ragged outline on this side than on its south-facing front, with many dense clumps thrusting out and as many small re-entrant glades and narrow paths leading through dense thickets. Any of these paths, natural entrances for deer seeking cover, might well have been taken by men leading tufters on their way to the drive.

Before going on I spent some moments at the south-western corner of the North wood. According to my estimate of how the hunt must have been organized, I believe that it was here the keeper of the Walk took his stand: just out of sight of any deer driven into the main glade from the wood's south face, but within reasonably close range—say twenty yards—of the first man of the presumed line of beaters. However, I had also supposed that the keeper's purpose in posting himself here was to receive from the Chief Hunter, standing with the King, the signal to start the drive. But from where I now stood—certainly the most logical place for the keeper to stand—I found that, looking east down the glade, I could no longer see the Rufus Stone; it was hidden by the North wood's southward bulge. For the signal to be visible to the keeper, the Chief Hunter would have to leave the King's side and move perhaps a score of yards to the south-west, to a point near the last of the existing trees in the grove. Even as I watched, a wandering

F

tourist in shirtsleeves chanced to pass the spot raising an arm to point; had he intended a signal I should have seen it clearly. No more than hypothetical, the keeper's imagined position squares with the facts of topography and the conditions of the hunt. (If the position is wrong, the action of the hunting is not affected; but in fact the action seems to assert that the position is right.)

There is little of interest to be seen on the western side, but I made sure by completing a circuit of the North wood. On a course that at first led me north-west over the broken heath I skirted the jutting thickets, making a few brief excursions into small winding glades to check the direction they took as much as to see whether, within, they afforded sufficient cover for deer. Gradually the course veered to north, to north-east, then sharply to east and past an open space of scrubby 'lawn' known as Upper Canterton Green. At length, after half an hour's plodding, I came back to the road just south of Upper Canterton and something like two hundred yards north of the Stone hidden by the trees. The time I had allowed myself was running short, but there was still one part of the task to be undertaken. Retracing my steps to the west, I turned south and into the North wood.

In it there has been, just as in those woods to the east of the road explored earlier, some thinning-out so that towards the centre, where I halted to get my bearings, the remaining trees are tall and widely spaced.[1] Judging the southern face of the wood to be between sixty and seventy yards away, I scouted around to find the best way through, encountering as I went a pair of schoolboys looking for a third and hunting about like a couple of terriers after a rabbit. The sight of them gave me an idea; because I noticed that, rather than thrust their way through dense undergrowth, each had found for himself a well-marked trail.

Following these trails in reverse, I now made two excursions from the centre to the wood's south face, checking the course by compass. The first trip took me along a narrow and winding path to a leafy opening—certainly a likely exit for driven deer—from

[1] See sketch-map, pages 72-3. My approximate position would be just north of the centre of the semi-circle of beaters.

The Rufus Stone seen from in front of 'Tirel's stand'; range approximately 90 yards. Autumn 1967. Sixty years ago the Stone would have been invisible from this point, due to the larger number of trees both to the right and in the centre of the picture, and to patches of holly and scrub. The foreground is marsh. The denudation of the area is due to the ever-increasing numbers of visitors, whose ceaseless tramping has destroyed the topsoil and thwarted natural regeneration.

Head of William Rufus, from a coin in the Ashmolean Museum, Oxford.

which I peered out across the glade, directly at the clump and notch on the face of the South wood. For the second trip I found a rather broader path, presently joined by others, all leading to the head of a deep bay. From this second exit I had an uninterrupted view south, across the 'lawn' to the steep slope that rises through gorse, bracken and stunted trees to meet the heath bordering the Stoney Cross road. A stag breaking cover from the bay would make for the slope ahead, for a gap between the shrubs that, as Cornish had observed seventy years earlier, is a natural pass for deer leaving the wooded hollow for the open highlands. Glancing half-left as I came out of the wood, I caught sight of the Rufus Stone; and, once again sliding about over sopping grass and oozing clay, I hurried towards it. Seventy paces I made it; call it sixty yards.

At the Stone I checked the time: five to seven by the sun. At this hour, in the year 1100, the first of the driven deer must have been coming out of the North wood, trotting timidly downwind into the glade. The sun would not set for a good thirty-five minutes, but already it hung low above the trees to the north of west and, facing the glade, I instinctively raised a hand to shield my eyes. So stood the King just before the end.

A quick glance at the compass, then I strode off (roughly south-south-west) to the limit of the trees. That not so long ago there were other trees in the grove is known, but those remaining are sufficient to allow an accurate reconstruction of the scene. Sixteen long paces I counted to beyond the last of them. As I halted and turned about, the corner of the South wood was over my shoulder; and when I looked back between the trees to the Stone I saw standing motionless beside it the figure of a man in a brown jacket—an unobstructed line of sight that brought for the smallest fraction of a second a desired illusion. It was not an unknown tourist whom I saw blinking at the sunset, but a thickset Norman with a red face. I could have shot him dead with almost any weapon.

IX

THE LORD OF POIX

WITH the journey of exploration still fresh in mind I made the first draft of my sketch-map to the honest scale of twenty yards to the inch. And here I must emphasise two points. First, that even in its final form it remains a *sketch*-map, an illustration to the text; at the same time, since both measurements and drawing were done with care, and with the help of the Ordnance Survey, the degree of accuracy is sufficient for calculations based upon the printed map's reduced scale to be correct to within two or three yards either way.

The second point is that I drew the map from notes taken during the first of several journeys, without reference to the story of the King's death; topography was not influenced by theory. Indeed so absorbed did I become in transferring to paper the things observed on the spot that for a time I almost forgot the object of the quest, the only point of historical detail inserted being the fixed point of the Rufus Stone of whose correct siting I no longer had any doubt.

One deviation from present reality has been allowed. About the Stone, from roughly east round to south, there have been 're-planted' some of those trees which, from the evidence of maps and photographs, are known to have stood in the grove in recent times. From other maps either ancient or modern little was to be gained. Nor did I believe, looking ahead, that aerial photographs could be of much assistance; they might help to delineate the woods more exactly; they could scarcely reveal the finer points in the hollow : the slopes, the marsh, the clay and the underlying gravel that confine the woods unalterably.

Only when the first reasonably satisfactory sketch was done did I refer back to the events described by the chroniclers, to see how theory might be fitted to the facts of topography. The King's position was accepted as known; possible, even probable, positions had been found for the seven hunters to the east, for the Chief Hunter not far from the King's side, for the keeper of the Walk and his party of beaters to the west. One man remained unplaced: Walter Tirel. To work out the most likely stand for for him to occupy, it will be best to consult again the relevant passages in the chroniclers' accounts.

William of Malmesbury, it will be remembered, says that 'the King was left alone with Walter Tirel'—alone, that is, with the necessary guides and attendants—that presently a stag 'passed near by', that the King shot at it and 'hit the mark but failed to kill'. A *second* stag passed by: 'Tirel shot at it and missed, but the arrow flew on and, by mischance, struck the King beyond.' With a small additional detail, Orderic Vitalis tells the same story. 'The King and Walter of Poix' were waiting in the wood. 'Suddenly a beast ran between them . . . and Walter let fly an arrow which shaved the hair on the animal's back, sped on and wounded the King.'[1]

The most obvious point common to both these accounts is that, although Tirel is held responsible, the King's death is seen as an accident. And although, among expert archers, shooting accidents must have been extremely rare, one might be tempted to leave it at that, were it not that on close examination there seems to be something wrong with the mechanics of the thing. The impression is that the King and Tirel were standing relatively close together; and the most probable place for Tirel to occupy on my map would therefore be the corner of the trees, some fifteen to twenty yards from the King, where previously I had put the Chief Hunter. This seemed rational enough—I had seen for myself

---

[1] Orderic says that the King, before being hit, 'jumped back from his place', but possibly he misunderstood the eyewitness account on this point. More probably the King's 'jump back' was the spasmodic movement of a man mortally wounded.

how easily a man at the Stone might be shot from that corner—
until I considered the behaviour of the *second* stag.

Was it likely or indeed conceivable that so alert yet timorous an
animal, driven from the North wood, should run towards that
same position to the east from which, a few moments earlier, its
fellow had been shot and was now fleeing to the west? Deer do
not rush upon known danger; but even supposing this second stag
to have been entirely unsuspecting, the natural course for it to
follow, on coming from the North wood, would be straight up the
open slope and through the pass to Stoney Cross moor. On this
course it could not run 'between' the King and Tirel. That could
only happen if Tirel were standing, not in the Chief Hunter's
place, but in the South wood.

The solution appeared so logical that I felt bound not to accept
it too hastily. Seeking an alternative, I tried upsetting my theory
of the hunt's organization by reversing the roles of the North and
South woods—imagining the direction of the wind to have been
not north-west but south-west. Although this completely destroyed
my carefully constructed eastern line of seven hunters, it did
enable Tirel to take a stand in the North wood at the same distance
from the King, fifteen to twenty yards, whilst the line of beaters
operated in the South wood. The trouble with this was that to be
sure of driving deer towards the King, the beaters would be
restricted to the extreme eastern edge of the wood, and that any
deer breaking cover on this side would be almost invisible to the
King either because of the trees south-west of his stand or because
of the sunlight. If, nevertheless, he did manage to shoot and
wound a stag it would certainly, because instinctively, turn towards the pass due south—which made nonsense of the story of the
King facing west and shielding his eyes against the sunset. It was,
of course, just possible that *one* of the deer driven from the South
wood should choose to turn north-east, come within bowshot of
the King and then, wounded, run off to the west. But it was quite
impossible to imagine a second stag following the path of the
first, still advancing when the other fled so that, coming eventu-

ally between the King and Tirel, it would cause them to shoot at one another.

To examine here the many other points that decided me against applying the theory 'in reverse' would be tedious and confusing. I went into them all, only to be forced back to my initial supposition that Tirel must have taken his stand somewhere on the eastern face of the South wood. And it was surprising how many factors seemed, at first, to support that belief. There was, however, some important evidence still to be taken into account— Tirel's own version of events.

Put into direct speech, what Tirel is reported to have said is simply this: 'I did not kill the King; I was in a different part of the wood that day; I did not see him at all during the hunt.' Before deciding on the merits of this statement which conflicts with the chroniclers' accounts, whether or not it agrees with the facts revealed by the topography of the woods, it will be wise to look more closely at the man himself.

What is known about him and his family is almost entirely due to the patient research of J. H. Round at the close of the 19th century. This shows that Walter was the third of his name to hold the lands of Poix.[1] His grandfather, Walter Tirel I, born either at the end of the 10th century or in the first decade of the 11th, is mentioned in a charter to Rouen cathedral in 1030. His father, Walter II, born around 1025-30, is named in a St Riquier charter of 1058 and again in a charter granted by Ralf, Count of Amiens, in 1069; he died probably before 1085. Walter III may have been born in about 1060; certainly he was married to Adelice (Alice) Clare before 1086, because in that year the Domesday survey shows that he had already been enfeoffed by his father-in-law, Richard Clare de Bienfaite, with the manor of Langham.

Alice's parents—her mother was Rohese, daughter of the elder Walter Giffard, the Conqueror's friend and comrade-in-arms— had founded St Neot's Priory, a cell to the Norman abbey of

---

[1] There was a Tirel at Hastings, but there appears to be no reliable evidence to establish his connection with Walter's family.

Bec, to which almost all the numerous Clare family contributed funds since the abbey stood on land held by their grandfather, Gilbert, Count de Brionne. The Tirels went further; not only did they contribute to Bec, where Alice's brother Richard was a monk, they founded the priory of St Denis de Poix and built the abbey of St Pierre at Sélincourt. Later in life they mortgaged part of the land of Langham to find further money for Bec; and on Walter's death—*circa* 1130—his only surviving son, Hugh, sold the manor to a wealthy London merchant, 'de Cornhill', and again gave the proceeds to Bec. This time it was probably to provide for his mother's last days, since she then retired to the nunnery at Conflans, an offshoot of Bec, where she died in 1138-9. Hugh continued as Lord of Poix and benefactor to Bec, and went on the second crusade in 1147.

From this, although no intimate portrait can be gained, there emerges the shadowy impression of a far from turbulent feudal lord, uninvolved in rebellion, attentive to the welfare of the Church in his own country, and holding considerable lands in Ponthieu (between Normandy and Flanders), lands that included Beaurain, Esquennes and Hesdin. Round notes that in the cartulary of Hesdin (in the Bibliothèque Nationale) it is written that Walter Tirel of Poix and his son Hugh made a free grant of houses to the village of Verton and, further, that they granted freedom of toll to Beaurain; from which one may deduce some administrative ability and a not ungenerous nature. At no time is there any suggestion of aggressive designs or of political intrigue.

For the rest, Walter appears to have been on good terms with the Clare family but to have taken no active interest in the affairs of England. There is no telling how often he visited Langham, or if he ever went there at all; he and his wife seem to have regarded the manor as little more than a valuable asset from which money could be raised when needed abroad. He may have met Rufus before August 1100—if so, then probably in France; but, 'a stranger at court', there is nothing to show that he was a close friend nor, *pace* Gaimar, who in rhyme but without reason hints at a plot, any evidence that he was a secret enemy. It may be supposed that he recognized as his feudal superior in England his brother-in-law Gilbert Clare, eldest son of Richard de Bienfaite, from whom he now held Langham; it is extremely unlikely that he, a Frenchman whose allegiance was to the count of Ponthieu, could thereby be drawn into a conspiracy whose object was regicide.

The one faint indication of Walter's appearance, is contained in that last scene just prior to the hunt when the King is said to have handed him a pair of arrows, naming him as 'the best shot'. An exceptional marksman then, but of relatively short stature; had he been much taller than the King the arrows, specially made for Rufus, would not have been long enough for Walter to draw effectively.[1]

On the strength of this rather tenuous record it cannot be said that Walter looks much like a murderer. Nor, supposing the King's death to have been accidental, does he look like a man who, from a safe distance and under no pressure, would deny strenuously, piously, and to the end of his life that he had had any share in the accident. What, however, most compels respect for his denial is the character of the man who recorded it : Suger, Abbot of St Denis, about whose reliability as a witness there can be no question.

Born in 1082 of poor parents, Suger was vowed to the abbey at the age of ten and studied there in the company of the son of Louis VI *le gros*. When, in 1137, that son became king as Louis VII, Suger acted as his minister—a post he had already held under his father—and when, ten years later, the king went crusading he was appointed regent of the kingdom of France. Meanwhile, in 1122, he had been elected abbot, and thereafter undertook, in addition to other labours at St Denis that included the rebuilding of the abbey, the writing of his *Life* of Louis VI. In this work, completed in about 1144, he related how he had 'often

---

[1] From the Conqueror's thigh-bone—all that remained of his body after various desecrations of the tomb at Caen over the centuries and which has since been lost—it was estimated that his height was at least five feet ten inches. Since several accounts refer to Rufus being 'shorter than' or 'not so tall' as his father, he was probably between five feet six and five feet eight. Walter Tirel may well have been about the same.

heard' Walter Tirel deny that he had taken any part in the death of Rufus; and he added that, on at least one occasion, the denial had been made in circumstances amounting to the taking of a sacred oath. Where this occurred does not seem to be known, but since Suger was only eighteen when Rufus was killed and did not become abbot until he was forty—when Tirel was within eight years of his death—he may have heard the solemn declaration, and others like it, in the course of visits to Bec or to some other of those religious houses to which Tirel was so constant a benefactor and, presumably, a fairly frequent visitor. Alternatively, or in addition, Tirel may have come to St Denis to give service to Louis VI at the time, 1119, of the unsuccessful campaign against Henry I in Normandy.

However this may be, it seems certain that Tirel's repeated declarations of innocence were made freely and with careful consideration before ecclesiastical witnesses. Independent confirmation comes from another reputable source. John of Salisbury, writing his *Life of St Anselm* in the second half of the 12th century, mentions that Tirel on his deathbed uttered a last and solemn protest against the charge of complicity in the King's death.

It is therefore strikingly clear from two trustworthy authorities that Tirel so deeply resented the charge against him—even when reduced to one of 'accidental' shooting—that for thirty years he continued, time after time and before God, to deny it. The very constancy of his denial, together with its simple wording, gives his testimony a strength far greater than that of any chronicler accusing him. In all the circumstances it is hard to see how that testimony can be regarded as anything but the truth.

Accepting Tirel's statement as true, I consulted the sketch-map to see how its wording corresponded with the topography. And saw at once that I had made a mistake in placing him on the eastern face of South Stricknage wood.

When Tirel said that he did not kill the King, he implied that he *could not* have killed him because he was 'in a different part of the wood', from which it was impossible to 'see the King at all.'

From the eastern face, although he could perhaps be said to be in a 'different part' of the wood, he must certainly have known beforehand where the King was standing, have seen him when the stag 'ran between' them and, at a range of sixty yards with the sun over his shoulder and shining upon the King, have been able to shoot him. Since, then, if we accept his statement, he cannot have stood upon the eastern face, he can only have stood upon the northern face. And in that case, where better than in the notch just behind the clump of trees discovered during my journey of exploration.

It would, of course, be wrong to insist too inflexibly upon the western side of the clump as the one and only spot where Tirel can have stood. His guide may have led him to the miniature glade some ten yards to the east; and there are other small indentations in the wood's north face that may have been rather more pronounced in Tirel's day and may then have served just as well. Yet the arguments in favour of the 'notch-and-clump' position are strong. First, it is there, and has been there for a very long time. Second, it would make, now as then, an excellent stand from which to shoot at deer driven from the North wood, its excellence only exceeded, as one might expect, by that of the King's stand. Third, it is unquestionably in a 'different part' of the wood and, from it, the position of the King (marked by the Stone) cannot be seen. Fourth, Tirel standing in the notch would be, at roughly ninety yards, well within bowshot of the King, but he could not possibly hit him, even if he wanted to, because of the intervening wall of trees.

What, however, finally decided me to accept the 'notch-and-clump' as the most probable position for Tirel to occupy was a fifth point : one that reconciles his statement with the chroniclers' accounts where many have seen a 'baffling contradiction'. But this point concerns the flight of the arrows and so is discussed more properly with the action of the hunt.

How Tirel reached his stand in the notch seems simple enough. He and the King must have parted company shortly after leav-

ing their horses near the Stoney Cross road. Then, whilst the
King and his attendant were conducted down into the hollow
amid the trees of the grove, Tirel and his attendant were led—
they must have been led or they would certainly have missed
the way—by one of the deer-paths through the denser thicket of
the South wood. The stand had no doubt been chosen with care,
probably by the Chief Hunter in conjuction with the keeper of
the Walk, and possibly with the approval of the King, who
according to Gaimar, treated the 'stranger at court' with 'special
favour'. As soon as Tirel had reached the place, the fact would
be signalled by his guide to the keeper at the western corner of
the North wood, just as a few moments earlier the Chief Hunter
had signalled the arrival of the King. With the last man of the
shooting party in his appointed position the drive could now
begin.

I should mention that on a subsequent exploration of the South
wood, begun from the back of the notch, I followed the ancient
deer-path leading through on a winding course approximately
south by east. Making my way along it for some fifty or sixty yards
uphill, I came out upon the scrubby heath not far from the deer-
pass to the ridge. Although there are other paths through the
wood, this seems the most likely one for Tirel's guide to have
chosen.

X

THE EARL OF TUNBRIDGE

THE search for clues to the character of Walter Tirel, Lord of Poix, in the light of the few known facts concerning him, brings one in due course to his brother-in-law Gilbert Clare who, as eldest son and successor to Richard de Bienfaite (son of Gilbert, Count of Brionne), was now Earl of Tunbridge. And placing the two men side by side one is struck by the contrast between them. The more closely one looks at each the farther does the tide of suspicion recede from Walter, the nearer does it flow towards Gilbert.

Not that Gilbert Clare himself could have shot the fatal arrow; one of the seven standing somewhere along the eastern shooting-line, he was out of bowshot of the King. Nor, save to establish his presence in the hunting party, does the documentary evidence prove his complicity in the crime, supposing the crime to have been murder. So strong, however, is the chain of circumstances suggesting a crime and involving him in it that it can scarcely be broken and never wholly be explained away.

Five pointers may be noted. Two of them concern character, two supply motive, and one the opportunity to conspire and to act.

1.   In the rebellion of 1088 Gilbert was involved against Rufus in favour of Robert. Nothing extraordinary about that; in this first testing year of the new reign almost all the barons rebelled; and then came quickly to heel when the King, loyally supported by the English fyrd (consisting of all males capable of bearing arms), moved resolutely against their leader Earl-Bishop Odo, and when the help promised by Robert failed to materialise. Nonetheless, Gilbert's first impulse had been to take arms against Rufus.

2. In 1095 he seems to have known well beforehand of the plot to kill the King and to replace him by Stephen of Aumale. Only at the last moment did he betray both plot and plotters to the King.

3. Almost all the members of both branches of the great and numerous Clare family, the sons and daughters of respectively Baldwin of Exeter and Richard of Tunbridge, were benefactors to the religious house at Bec and to its offshoots in England. It will be remembered that Gilbert's father, Richard, had founded St Neot's Priory, to which his mother, Rohese Giffard, was a benefactress; his brother Walter, moreover, was later to found Tintern Abbey, and his brother Richard, due for speedy promotion, was already a monk at Bec. Although these many associations with the Church are not, since they were the normal practice of the day, to be regarded as evidence of exceptional piety—even Rufus contributed to the support of the abbey at Battle founded by his father, and himself founded a monastery at Bermondsey—they prove at least a continuing family interest in the Church's welfare, as much in England as in Normandy. Earl Gilbert, head of his branch of the Clares, must certainly have known of the Church's numerous grievances, of the king's exactions at variance with feudal custom, of the bishoprics and abbacies held vacant, of the disputes that had kept Anselm in exile for four years while the King enjoyed the revenues of the see and of the monks of Canterbury.

Since no lifting of the Church's burden was to be expected during the King's lifetime it may have seemed to Gilbert that the lifetime might be shortened with advantage. To one sympathetic to the Church's cause, moved perhaps by that angry resentment doubtless expressed by the ecclesiastic members of his family, the righting of the Church's just complaints may well have provided a motive for violent action. Open rebellion was out of the question; the King was too strong. But we are entitled to think that Gilbert, who had already been involved in two plots to remove the King, would scarcely be averse to planning a third, at once more direct in its aim and more effective in its execution.

4. Gilbert seems to have been on good terms with Henry before 1100 as well as afterwards; for one possible reason because the King's cupbearer Eudo *dapifer*, known to be the firmest of Henry's friends, had married Rohese Clare, the elder of Gilbert's two sisters. (The other sister, Alice Tirel, was the youngest of the family of seven.) But if it was Gilbert who helped to plan the removal of the King and who thus so greatly advanced Henry's fortunes, one would expect something more than friendly terms; one would look, after the event, for rewards and favours to the Clares. And rewarded and favoured they were. All modern historians have noted the fact and perceived its significance. Only one thing has seemed puzzling : that Tirel, generally regarded as the individual directly responsible for the King's death, should not have been rewarded personally either by Henry or by the Clares. Once it is appreciated, however, that it was not Tirel who shot the fatal arrow, and that this was known to the conspirators, it becomes plain that he got nothing because he did nothing. The rewards were intended by Henry for those of the Clares—and their close relatives, the Giffards—who had actively supported him.

In these rewards, some of which must surely have been agreed beforehand to judge from the exceptional speed of their granting, there may be discerned a further motive inducing Earl Gilbert to plot the death of Rufus. He may also have forseen additional rewards, to be gained in Normandy, were Henry to supplant both Rufus and Robert.

5. The question of opportunity seems at first to be hardly worth examining. Any of the King's close companions could find, in the course of an informal hunting party, some easy way to kill the man who trusted them. With a relatively small court, a correspondingly reduced bodyguard and vigilance relaxed, a secret enemy among the 'friends' would find no difficulty in nocking on an arrow, drawing in the bow and shooting to kill, all in a matter of seconds. To this, however, the great objection would be that it could be regarded only as murder; and the appearance of murder was something to be avoided at all costs. The bishops, upon whom Henry counted for support, could not possibly approve openly

the deliberate assassination of a King who, hateful though he might have become, was still their rightful lord and the Lord's anointed. The barons, by no means all of whom were friendly to Henry, would be up in arms either to seize what advantage they could in the anarchy ensuing upon the King's violent death or to take sides against the younger brother in favour of the elder, the legitimate heir Robert. Even the people, the cowed voiceless English, would hang back from supporting a known murderer. And abroad the repercussions might be serious. Murder was ruled out; an 'accident' it had to be.

How to make it plausible? It would seem likely in the hunting-field; even more likely in the New Forest where already the Conqueror's second son, Richard, and a bastard son of Robert's had met with fatal accidents; where, moreover, the Church, if it swallowed the tale of 'mischance', could give it additional colour by depicting the event as divine retribution both for the King's blasphemies and for his and his father's supposed destruction of churches in the district. And to Henry, supposing him to have been the arch-conspirator, the Forest offered a paramount advantage over other hunting lands: it lay close to Winchester and the vitally important Treasury.

An accident, then, in the New Forest. But who was to encompass it? A skilled hunter was required, expert in all things connected with Forest hunting, a knight-huntsman in whose discretion the conspirators might place absolute confidence, whose rank would allow him to approach the King, whose authority would protect him from interference; and the one man in all the hunting-court fully equipped to meet these requirements would be the Chief Hunter. How he was drawn into the plot can only be guessed; it may be that he held some ancient grudge against the King and that he was talked over with much the same inducements that may have moved Gilbert Clare: the righting of the Church's grievances and the promise of some personal reward. It may also be that he was related to Clare or Giffard; among the two hundred or so Norman families established in England some relationship, by blood or by marriage, was seldom far to seek.

In secret conclave with Gilbert—perhaps also with Henry but more probably, because more safely, alone with Gilbert—he would be able to say without much hesitation that yes, he could arrange to shoot the King easily enough in the course of a deer hunt and that no one would see him do it; but that if the shooting was to appear 'accidental' then careful planning would be necessary. Some other hunter, he may have suggested, must be so placed as to shoot, and be seen to shoot, towards the King; someone who could not possibly be suspected of wanting to kill him; preferably an honoured guest whom the King would himself have invited to take the stand nearest to him.

For such a plan to work, one of the King's companions must be framed—not for murder, for the 'accident'—and had any baron in England been chosen it would be necessary to seek other conspirators and other motives. But as soon as Walter Tirel appears on the scene there is no need to look elsewhere. Who more appropriate than the Lord of Poix?—a Frenchman rich, powerful and respected in his own country, who had seldom if ever visited England, who was in no way involved in the affairs of the kingdom and could have no reason whatever for murdering the King. Who better placed to invite him than his brother-in-law, Earl Gilbert? Roger, the other Clare brother included in the hunting party, seems to have been living in Normandy at this time (possibly at Brionne, possibly at Bec to which he was a constant benefactor); if so, conveying the invitation, he may have accompanied Walter to England.

Stripped of conjecture, the five points of circumstantial evidence present a formidable total. Character, motive, opportunity, the 'accident' blamed upon a relative who dwelt beyond the jurisdiction of both England and Normandy, the decisive support given subsequently to the dead King's successor, all point unerringly at Gilbert Clare, Earl of Tunbridge. Whether or not the inducements held out by Henry weighed more than the secret promptings of resentful prelates is of little consequence; Gilbert remains the man most likely to have planned the murder of the King.

XI

THE THREE ARROWS

SUFFICIENT evidence has now been gathered to permit a reconstruction of the crime. To follow this on the spot it will be best to revisit first the clump-and-notch stand on the face of the South wood, and then to return to the last of the trees south-west of the Rufus Stone. With the help of the sketch-map the exact sequence of events can then be worked out.

It will be remembered that the time of the King's arrival at his stand was reckoned to be some five or ten minutes before seven o'clock. Tirel, with a slightly longer path to follow, may have come into the notch a minute or two later. Their arrivals having been signalled, for the King by the Chief Hunter, for Tirel by his forest guide, the keeper of the Walk (western corner, North wood) gave the order to the nearest beater. Word was then passed on from man to man and the line moved forward; the drive had begun.

Allowing for the density of the cover, for the cautious advance of the beaters while the tufter hounds worked stealthily ahead, some five minutes must have passed before the first of the deer broke cover. (It should be repeated that no separate estimate need be made for the eastern line of seven hunters; the drive there, though starting at approximately the same time as that for the King, would go on independently and could in no way affect the action to the west.) It was thus at between five minutes to seven and seven o'clock when two stags, roughly fifty yards apart, came trotting out of the North wood and headed upon converging courses for the south pass.

What happened next took place in a matter of seconds, perhaps fifteen seconds in all, probably less. Inevitably, it must take much longer than that to describe; but if, from this point on, all words indicative of surmise have been omitted it is not merely for the sake of brevity, but because conjecture seems to be excluded since no other sequence appears possible. Three factors tend to prove this : topography, Tirel's statement, and the records of the chroniclers who, reporting an eyewitness account, were misled, as was the eye-witness himself, upon a single and vital point—the number of arrows shot.

The first stag to appear came from the more westerly of the two paths. When first seen by Tirel it presented a difficult target, head-on at the rather excessive range for a lethal shot of sixty yards. But since, from the notch, the light was good he allowed it to advance on its instinctively chosen course towards the south pass, hoping to put in a flank shot at closer range when it came to the centre of the main glade, which it would reach in from six to eight seconds depending on its speed. With arrow nocked on the string he waited. (Alternatively, he may have hoped that the stag would turn west, up the glade. But, given the habitual use made of the south pass and given also the beaters and hounds closing in from the west whom the stag must have winded, this turn was most improbable.)

The other stag, breaking cover only seconds after Tirel's, came out of the bay nearest the King. It, too, offered a difficult target head-on at sixty yards. Normally the King would have waited, as Tirel was waiting, for the stag to come broadside on at half the range; and had the hunt commenced an hour earlier he would almost certainly have delayed for, say, twenty seconds for an easy shot on the flank. Had he, even then, only wounded the beast it would have fled south; and the Chief Hunter, standing—presumably, with arrow already nocked on—at the corner of the grove would have brought it down as it went by him. (Had the Chief Hunter missed the mark, the stag would have continued to run south and would then have been intercepted by the huntsman almost certainly guarding the pass with hounds.) But at this sunset hour no delay was possible; with every forward pace the stag came nearer to the line of blinding light. For the King it was now or not at all. Drawing in his bow, he shot obliquely at fifty yards' range. Some four or five seconds had elapsed since the sighting; six or seven since Tirel's sighting.

Almost simultaneously Tirel drew and shot. That he cannot have waited longer is plain because his stag was still heading south-east, unaffected by the spring to the west of the King's stag, now wounded. With his (Tirel's) stag past the centre-line of the glade the range had shortened to forty yards, but with its next few strides the quarry would be lost to sight, eclipsed by the wall of trees. A forced shot, the arrow quite possibly deflected by the cross-wind, he missed narrowly. Whether or not the arrow 'shaved the hair' on the animal's back, as Orderic reported, it is unlikely to have flown on more than a score of yards at most before dropping harmlessly upon the open 'lawn'. The stag, alarmed but unhurt, fled uphill towards the south pass, running 'between the King and Tirel'.

The King, meanwhile, was watching his own stag. The arrow had hit, but upon the obliquely-presented target the wound was slight. Stung and terrified the animal sprang away. It could not turn back into the North wood whence it had been driven by the scent and sound of danger; it could not hold to the south whence had come the arrow. Its only course to safety lay westward, up the glade towards Fritham Plain, straight into the sunset. For some five to seven seconds the King stood motionless, bowhand dropped, right hand raised to shield his eyes. And it was then that the Chief Hunter, having seen Tirel's arrow fly and fall, and Tirel's stag run south, turned with a fateful five seconds to spare; drew, aimed between the stems of the trees and, at the range of under twenty yards, shot the King.

The only point of divergence between this account and those of William of Malmesbury and of Orderic Vitalis concerns the number of arrows flown. Both chroniclers agree on this point: the King loosed one arrow, which wounded a stag, and Tirel loosed one, which missed a stag and struck the King. Later chroniclers follow the same line: only two arrows, and Tirel's killed the King.

Upon reflection, this is seen to be impossible. Topography, supporting Tirel's unequivocal three-point statement, rules it out. By no conceivable means could Tirel, standing within the northern face of the South wood, shoot to kill the King whether by accident or by design. Even allowing for a strong cross-wind and for the further deflection (hinted by Orderic) caused by 'shaving the hair' on the stag's back, the shot is still impossible; the arrow, after first flying some forty yards, would have to turn through almost forty-five degrees and then speed on for another fifty yards before hitting the King. An arrow is not like a bullet fired from a rifle, that may ricochet from a hard surface and still fly on to inflict mortal injury at some considerable distance. Any obstruction sufficient to deflect an arrow through a sharp angle will so reduce its momentum that it can but fall harmlessly within a few feet. The later story that the arrow glanced from the oak-tree near the King fails for the same reason. Of course any sharp-pointed missile, however slowly moving, might injure or put out an eye. Only a direct shot from close range could strike 'straight to the heart' with such force as to cause instant death.

To sum up. Whether Tirel stood back in the notch or forward and just within the clump—a difference of at most fifteen feet, which may be increased or reduced, here as elsewhere, by ten per cent to allow for marginal fluctuation of the woods over the years —his line of sight towards the King was blocked by the trees of the South wood. His arrow cannot have turned the corner of these trees save by a deflection that must have deprived it of all penetrative power. It cannot have flown directly to the mark; had it sped straight on after missing the stag altogether it would have passed some thirty yards to the north of the King's position. Since, therefore, it was not Tirel's arrow that killed the King, and since the King's own arrow is known to have wounded a stag, death can only have been caused by a third arrow. And the only person within lethal range who can have shot this arrow is the man who stood at the corner of the grove south-west of the King. He it was who knew exactly where Tirel was posted, who knew the direction in which Tirel would have to shoot given the south-easterly course of the deer driven towards the King and instinctively seeking to escape by the south pass, and who, after the fall of Tirel's arrow and the flight of his stag, knew that in fact Tirel had shot and missed. He alone had the opportunity; it came during those few seconds while the King stood motionless and half-blinded by the setting sun.

XII

THE BOW AND THE BOWMAN

ALLOWING for possible errors either way of two or three seconds' time and a few yards' distance, the account of the manner in which the King was killed represents what must actually have happened. But one must also consider what might have been expected to happen; because it was obviously impossible for the Chief Hunter—who on other occasions elsewhere in the Forest may have been biding his time for days—to know beforehand that Tirel, on this very evening, would shoot only one arrow and, with it, miss the target so helpfully. What he, the Chief Hunter, most probably counted upon was that, with the lateness of the hour compelling the beaters to close in swiftly, three or four stags would be driven into the glade in fairly rapid succession; that in a matter of, say, thirty seconds to a minute the King and Tirel between them would loose at least as many arrows as there were stags running; that most of them would hit, but one or two miss; and that in the confusion of arrows flying on various courses the desired opportunity would arise. It was the chance that Tirel missed with his first shot, in the general direction of the King, that brought the opportunity forward.

The idea of a confusion of arrows leads to the conjecture that back at the Lodge the Chief Hunter might have obtained a new arrow similar to the half-dozen the King had received from his armourer. It seems probable that the armourer would have more than just six new shafts in his keeping, and that a man of the Chief Hunter's standing would be able to lay hands on one without arousing comment or being observed. Using it to kill the King he would then be able to point to the broken shaft lying beside the body and say : 'Look!—is it not one of those the King gave to the Lord of Poix?'

A surmise, no doubt; but wilder ones have sometimes been accepted upon even flimsier evidence. I came across one, in which a number of responsible people seem firmly to believe, at the very start of my inquiry. It concerns the weapon with which the King was killed. This, it is said, was not an arrow from a long-bow but a bolt from a cross-bow.

Who first gave currency to this theory is not certain. It may have been due in the first place to a word inserted by Orderic Vitalis in his account of events at the Lodge just before the King rode out. It will be remembered how he says that it was while the King dressed for the hunt that the armourer came to present the six new arrows of which two were given to Tirel; only instead of using the word *sagitta* he substituted, for once, *catapulta*. And it appears to have been this one word—I can find no other reason —that led Hugh Ross Williamson first to imagine a cross-bow and then, briefly describing the shooting of the King in *The Arrow and the Sword*,[1] to go further and declare that 'the arrow was one of two special ones, designed not for the cross-bow but for the more deadly arbalest'. No evidence is offered in support of the statement, and none appears to exist; yet some have come to accept it, or at least the cross-bow theory, as proven fact.

Before setting out on the quest, I asked the Royal Toxophilite Society for technical information on the range, power and accuracy of the long-bow, and I then learned of a number of people who held that the arguments in favour of the cross-bow were 'overwhelming'. Summarized, they amount to this: 1. The shooting of the King could have been done more easily with a cross-bow than with a long-bow. 2. A cross-bow can be carried 'loaded' for an indefinite period, whereas the long-bow can be held drawn for no more than a few seconds. 3. The cross-bow is more easily handled and requires little clear space behind cover for raising it to the aiming position, whilst the long-bow

[1] Faber, 1955.

needs twice the space to ensure that neither of its limbs touch a branch or a twig on being loosed. 4. A long-bow demands more skill, practice and strength to aim accurately than does a cross-bow.

Although these arguments are based on nothing more substantial than the supposedly superior merits of the cross-bow, coming from experienced archers they are not be scorned. They are best countered, in the first place, by a careful scrutiny of the early chroniclers.

In relating the events concerning the hunt and the death of the King, William of Malmesbury, Orderic Vitalis—his one mention of *catapulta* apart—the Anglo-Saxon chronicler and Geoffrey Gaimar all refer to a bow and arrow, the first two using *arcus* and *sagitta* for which Gaimar uses the old French derivative *sajete*; and in this context William and Orderic between them use *sagitta* more than half a dozen times. Conceivably, however, it might be objected that 'arrow' was a general term applied to any missile-weapon—as we might loosely write today that a man had been shot with 'a gun' without specifying whether it was a pistol, rifle or twelve-bore. To make sure, I hunted through the Latin and English sources to see if either *sagitta* or arrow was invariably used for any kind of shooting. The search was revealing.

Of a man shot in Normandy in the Conqueror's time (1079) the Anglo-Saxon chronicler writes: 'he was killed by a bolt from a crossbow.' Dealing with the death of Rufus he says: 'killed by an arrow'. Similarly William of Malmesbury, relating the death (1106) of a tenant well known in the see of Worcester, says that the veteran Roger of Gloucester *'in obsessione falesiae arcubalistae jactu in capite percussum'*—hit in the head by 'a bolt from a crossbow' at the siege of Falaise; but about Rufus he says that he was hit in the breast by 'an arrow' *(sagitta)*. Elsewhere Orderic makes the same careful distinction; so that from these and other examples it seems clear that when the chroniclers used the word *sagitta*, and used it repeatedly, they meant just that; conversely, when a bolt from a cross-bow was the missile employed they said so.

What appears to strengthen the argument is William of Malmesbury's description of the King's death. The arrow struck and *'clutching at the shaft* where it protruded from his breast the King fell forward, *breaking the arrow* as he hit the ground'. It seems unlikely that either of those two telling phrases could apply to the much shorter and stouter bolt from a cross-bow.

A further point is to be gleaned from internal evidence in the chroniclers' accounts. William, Orderic, Gaimar, and those who followed later, all show the King and Tirel 'drawing bows' and 'loosing arrows' at the driven deer. The sudden intrusion of a single cross-bow, of a bolt from it striking the King, would have been so extraordinary an incident that it could not possibly have escaped the attention of those present. The implication of deliberate shooting then patent to all would have destroyed utterly the 'accident' theory which could only be credited if all the hunters, Tirel and the Chief Hunter included, were using the same weapon. And that it should be credited was vital to the plot's success.

One last point. Not even with the help of a cross-bow could Tirel have hit the King from the position where, within a few yards either way, he undoubtedly stood.

Without prejudicing the case by revealing in advance my own view of the manner in which Rufus was killed, I next asked the Royal Toxophilite Society a number of questions concerning the use of the long-bow. I wanted to discover whether the Chief Hunter's task, however strong the circumstantial evidence supporting it, was in fact technically feasible.

Could he, I asked, be sure of killing with a single arrow? He would not, for obvious reasons, be able to shoot twice. From the fact, attested by William of Malmesbury and Orderic, that the King died almost instantaneously on being hit it seemed certain, as Gaimar says, that the arrow went 'straight to the heart'—a mark only three to four inches in diameter. Could it be done, given the range? Sixteen yards I made it from the end of the trees; it may well have been nearer twenty, with the greater number of trees that were there in the past. Above all, could it be done in the strictly limited time? The King, according to William of Malmesbury, stood watching the wounded stag 'for some time'; how long was that? I had tried it myself; stood motionless at the Stone, looking west, hand raised to my eyes against the sunset on the equivalent date. Six or seven seconds seemed a reasonable maximum, given the speed of the running stag. But the assassin would have less than that. He had to hold his shot until, with Tirel's stag running towards the pass, Tirel's arrow could be seen flying out from the South wood; because unless Tirel did shoot, and shoot in the general direction of the King, there could be no subsequent pretence of an accident. Was the speed with which the waiting bowman would then have to act attainable even by a skilled marksman? He may have had five or six seconds, perhaps only four.

These are the answers with which the Royal Toxophilite Society was good enough to supply me.

1. There is no doubt about the killing power of a suitable arrow shot from a suitable bow. (Not all cross-bows would have a greater range or more killing power than a hunting, or war, long-bow.)
2. It is certain that there are bowmen capable of hitting a small mark, say three inches in diameter, virtually every time at a range of twenty to thirty yards.
3. Provided the archer already had his arrow nocked on the string, four seconds would be ample time for a skilled hunter to draw, aim, and loose. The time of flight would be around a quarter-second at the range suggested (twenty yards), initial velocity being somewhere about 250-300 feet per second.

Armed with these clearcut statements I went over the culminating events of the tragedy with the help and advice of one who had been my companion on earlier visits. And in passing I should explain that this patient friend—who ruined a pair of shoes that day trudging through the marsh—was not only a competent archer and something of an athlete, but also a forester born and the son of born foresters. Quick to appreciate any point of reasonable conjecture, he was as quick to reject any point that seemed to him improbable by reason of his sense of history, his knowledge of archery, and his almost instinctive awareness of what might or might not happen in the special conditions pertaining to the New Forest.

Together we fixed upon a number of probabilities that seemed to come very near to the exact truth. First, in the pre-arranged plan of action the bowman-assassin—leaving aside the problem of his identity for the time being—knew that the King would be facing the North wood whence the deer were to be driven. When the time came it would matter little whether or not the King himself had already loosed an arrow; motionless, watching intently, he would present a sure mark to the man on his left flank. Second, the bowman would certainly know that Walter Tirel, the 'honoured guest' (Gaimar) and 'best shot' (Orderic), had been allotted a nearby stand in the South wood, from which he would be compelled to shoot obliquely towards the King—compelled because, although a single stag might escape to the west, it was naturally towards the King their master that the beaters would be driving the deer whose instinct, once they had broken cover, would lead them south. Once Tirel's arrow had flown, and been seen to fly—by his own men, incidentally, as well as by the bowman—the opportunity arose, brief but expected. And the rest, by the considered opinion of experts in archery, was relatively easy. It was made easier by the chance that the King, having shot, inclined more and more to his left until, after five or six seconds, he faced directly into the sun. Dazzled by the light, yet offering a broader target, neither he nor his attendant could see the assassin as he drew in his bow.

One detail I had overlooked. Concentrating upon the three arrows I had forgotten the two stags and the number of men who must have been watching them. The huntsman whom I had placed with a couple of hounds—a reasonable guess—on the edge of the grove, guarding the south pass, watched Tirel's stag as it ran 'between' Tirel and the King (Orderic). The King and his attendant archer watched the wounded stag 'running west' (William of Malmesbury). Tirel, too, having lost sight of his own stag, must have watched the wounded animal from the notch, his guide and his attendant watching with him. Perhaps he shot at it; but, if so, he may well have missed so fast-moving a mark as it galloped up Gaimar's 'marsh' towards Leland's 'Fritham'. Next it would be watched by the keeper of the Walk and, across the glade, by the huntsman at the western corner of the South wood, who may then have slipped his 'hounds to hunt uphill' (Peter Blois). So it was that from all sides men, eight or nine in all, watched the quarry. No one watched the bowman who, safely and almost at leisure, could draw, aim and shoot to kill.

That the assassin stood at the approximate end of the trees to the south-west of the King's position seems to be proved by four independent considerations. First, it is clear from the chroniclers' accounts that the King was shot from in front; in the breast, not in the back. Second, from the sureness of the aim at a small mark, the shortness of time available and the penetrative force required, it appears certain that the arrow was shot from a range of no more than twenty yards and probably less. Third, from no other point can the arrow have been shot : line of sight, angle, range, or all three together, rule it out. Fourth, by the unchanging nature of the soil in the hollow there can never have been sufficient undergrowth at this corner of the grove to conceal some other, unknown assassin or to permit a stranger's unseen approach from any of the denser thickets. That Tirel did not shoot the fatal arrow is proved as much by his own repeated denials as by the unaltering topography of the woods and by the instinctive and unvarying behaviour of driven deer facing danger. For to repeat a point already examined in detail, had it been Tirel, and not the bowman, who was posted at the corner of the grove, it would be inconceivable that the 'second stag' should advance when the first had fled, to pass 'between' him and the King.

From these many points some confirmation had been gained of the assassin's presumed identity. Clearly he was one of the relatively few entitled to carry a bow during the hunt—apart, that is, from the King and his friends. To be authorized to stand near the King, openly and unquestioned, he must have been an official of rank, a knight-huntsman. The enormity of what he did the knowledge that enabled him to act with speed and decision when the opportunity arose, and the significant circumstance that he was neither accused nor suspected of the crime, all suggest strongly that he was the principal organizer of the King's hunting; at the very least a deputy to the man known by the Norman title then equivalent to Chief Hunter.

From lack of evidence he remains a man without a face; but not necessarily a man without a name. Late in the 12th century Gerald of Wales, though not denying the story of 'mischance', wrote (in *De Instructione Principum*) that the man who shot the King was one *'Ranulf de Aquis'*—which leaves one to imagine what he was called in everyday life. All monkish chroniclers went in for a confusing latinization of men's place-names, and Gerald of Wales went farther than most. For instance, he renders the name of Montmorency as *'de monte mauricii'*, which seems a long way from the humble hamlet whence the family originated and whose early spelling is given as 'Mumerci'. Not that this sort of embellishment casts doubt upon his reliability as a chronicler; a remarkably well-informed observer, who had, as Poole says, 'studied at Paris and Oxford, had travelled far and seen much of the world', he was also a prolific writer. In his *Gemma Ecclesiastica*—a work that, if it scandalized some, was enjoyed by many a prelate: it is said the Pope kept a copy at his bedside—he depicted, with an ironic wit exceptional for the period, the life and character of the English parish priest of his day. A picture true enough, even though the Church termed it exaggerated; for the parish priest was often, in Poole's words, 'grossly illiterate, with scarcely enough Latin to repeat the church services correctly'; a man so ill rewarded that he took for himself the money paid for masses; one, moreover, who, in Gerald's neat phrase, 'kept a hearth-girl *(focaria)* who kindled his fires but extinguished his virtue'.

That so lively and knowledgeable a writer, whose accuracy

is accepted by modern historians, should have chosen for the man who killed the King a name at random seems highly improbable, out of keeping with the responsible character revealed by his writings. What seems more likely is that the name of the killer was already known to other and earlier writers who shrank from telling it in view of the officially disseminated story which could not be gainsaid without peril. It was not only that Gerald had the necessary boldness, but that, by the time he wrote, more than fifty years had passed since the death of Rufus and the name no longer mattered much. Nor was this the first occasion on which Tirel's name had been omitted; 'The King was killed by an arrow shot by one of his men,' the Anglo-Saxon chronicler had written shortly after the event. No mention there of any 'accident'; and none of Tirel, since not even by an unwarrantable stretching of his position as sub-tenant to Earl Gilbert could the Lord of Poix be termed one of the King's men. But whether or not the English chronicler was aware of the killer's identity, the fact remains that Gerald's account is the first to mention a name other than Tirel's and that by the time the account was published Abbot Suger's *Life of Louis le Gros*, containing Tirel's solemn denial, was already well known. It may even be wondered whether, towards the close of the 12th century, any man versed in the political history of his time still believed either in the tale of 'mischance' or in Walter Tirel's guilt.

Since Gerald's accuracy is not impugned the name he gives deserves a brief scrutiny. *Ranulf*—the English Ralph and French Raoul—seems then to have been in more common use in Normandy than in England or elsewhere. *Aquis*, it may reasonably be supposed, stands for one of the many Roman *Aquae* corrupted to *Aix* and linked to some place containing mineral springs. Perhaps more frequently then than now the plural article preceded the place-name, as in *les Aix d'Angillon* near Bourges. But it is no use guessing from which of the many *Aix* the man hailed; there is no evidence. It is possible, but this is only a conjecture, that his name presently came to be written in French as one word, in a form fairly widespread and seven centuries later to become famous in military history: *Desaix*.[1] At all events, it is permissible to imagine, provided that the name is followed by a question-mark, that the bowman who killed Rufus was a Norman knight-huntsman known as Raoul des Aix de ——? Conceivably, he may have been related to one or other of the conspirators. Failing new evidence it can scarcely be brought nearer than that, and it will be safer to continue to refer to him by the latinized name supplied by Gerald of Wales: *Ranulf de Aquis*.

[1] Louis Desaix de Veygoux, gallant and supremely competent general, killed at Marengo after converting to victory Bonaparte's defeat, June 1800.

XIII

THE DUPE AND HIS COUNSELLOR

SEEN from the conspirators' point of view, the murder was a skilful piece of work: three arrows in quick succession, the King's, Tirel's, the Chief Hunter's, the last fatal, and all over in a matter of seconds. Not the least skilful part of it was the manner in which the Chief Hunter's arrow came from so nearly the same direction as Tirel's that it might easily be mistaken for it by an observer who could not see clearly because of the sun.

This must surely have been the first impression upon the mind of the archer-attendant standing behind the King in that fearful moment when the arrow struck. An impression that, momentarily effaced by the greater horror of seeing the King drop dead at his feet, may well have been recalled a few moments later by the assassin himself. Because, at the man's first cry of dismay, the Chief Hunter must have come striding up—to put, even as he gazed at the body, a natural yet cunning question: Whence did the arrow come? To which the King's man can only have answered: from over there, to the left. This the Chief Hunter could at once confirm: had he not seen a stag run south, seen an arrow fly and miss? An arrow that, flying on, must have struck the King 'by mischance'. To the King's man this would seem, just then, to be the only possible explanation; he too may have glimpsed Tirel's stag but intent on staring against the sun after the King's stag, he can scarcely have seen the harmless fall of Tirel's arrow. For him there were only two arrows: the one the King had shot, and the one that had killed the King. Since Tirel was the only member of the hunting party within bowshot to the west, that second arrow must have been his. Any puzzled doubts he might then express would be countered by the Chief Hunter's own opinion, coupled, it may be, to the warning that he had better stick to his story or he might himself be suspected of the shooting.

Less than half a minute can have been spent in anxious exclamation before both men turned to raise the alarm, their sudden shouts echoing through the silent woods, conveying by their very tone some immediate intimation of disaster; drawing within short minutes a hurrying crowd of hunters and huntsmen, and presently the seven 'great men' from the shooting-line to the east; all to assemble in varying degrees of real or simulated consternation about the spot where the King lay dead. To them the King's man, however unnerved and distraught, told his brief eye-witness story.

Nothing seems more clearly to prove the existence of the King's personal attendant than the account given by William of Malmesbury. No one other than a man standing close by the King could have supplied details so vivid that, surviving translation into Latin and re-translation into English, they still carry conviction. At only one point can the least lameness be detected in the story's dramatic precision, a point where the witness seems momentarily to falter. Unaware of the third arrow, he accepts the impossible chance of the second, but—an archer himself—accepts it reluctantly at, one must suppose, the prompting of the Chief Hunter who alone can have added the detail about the arrow 'shaving the hair on the animal's back', since he alone had seen the harmless fall of Tirel's arrow.

Others too there must have been, out of the score of hunters, huntsmen and hunt-servants, presently gathered about the body, who distrusted the 'mischance' theory, who shook their heads but only later whispered their suspicions. Geoffrey Gaimar seems to have heard something of this gossip because, after repeating the accepted story that 'by an evil fate' Tirel's arrow struck the King and 'went straight to his heart', he makes a startling admission that brings him very near to the truth. Put in plain English, and for once he abandons his poetic embroidery, this is what he says, with my italics: 'We *do not know* who shot the arrow. But this said *the other archers*, that it came from Walter's bow. And it *seemed* like it because he immediately fled.'

Mention of 'the other archers' shows that at least two men stood close to the King. But their testimony that Tirel had shot the arrow was little more than an expression of opinion, since it relied upon Tirel's flight for confirmation. But if Tirel was innocent, as he appeared to be and later so strenuously claimed, why did he run?

In the course of events subsequent to the King's death time and distance are such decisive factors that, lining up the known facts, it would not be impossible to plot a graph; one on which miles against minutes fix the curve with such certainty that any reasonable surmise fitting into the close pattern can be regarded as probably accurate; there is neither space nor time for serious error. And it is in the shortness of time between successive events that the clearest evidence can be found of a long-premeditated conspiracy.

For how long, one may begin by wondering, did the members of the hunting party remain at that spot on the fringe of the grove where the King had fallen? Certainly not as long as Geoffrey Gaimar suggests in his poetic description of weeping and wailing, of foresters wielding axes to cut down and measure up branches for a bier, of others gathering flowers and ferns to make a scented couch for the corpse, of grooms leading richly-caparisoned palfreys to bear away the body while sorrowing barons walk sadly beside it. The time-factor forbids such prolonged ceremonial.

At the other extreme the impression given by many historians that no instructions whatever were given for the care of the body is surely incredible. After all, the dead man had been King for thirteen years and to some at least in the narrow circle of his companions he had been a true friend, chivalrous, boisterously good-humoured, lavishly generous. To the majority who were not in the conspiracy the very suddenness of his violent end in these peaceful surroundings must have come as a bewildering shock. Nor should the characteristics common to the members of the hunting party be forgotten. These men were not 'English', stolid, taciturn, submissive; they were Normans, at the zenith of Norman power and genius, headstrong, impulsive, at times emotional. At the first sight of their lord the King stretched inert at their feet, distress must have been immediate, voluble and sincere.

At least for most of them. Gaimar may be romancing when he makes Robert fitz-Hamon—apparently the first to arrive on the scene—cry out for someone to end his life since he has now nothing to live for; but it does not sound impossible, any more than does the mild stroke or fainting-fit from which he is then said to have suffered. He was perhaps the King's closest and most loyal friend; seeing him dead he may well have felt that the whole meaning and purpose of his life had been destroyed. Others in varying degree may have felt much the same. The Treasurer, William of Breteuil, probably, and Gilbert of Laigle too. Even Henry, whatever his secret thoughts concerning his brother, must have found it expedient just then to express an extremity of sorrow. He seems, fom Gaimar's account, to have been the last to come up; he may have chosen to stand at the eastern end of the line, where he could not be suspected of the shooting.

But hard upon the initial explosion of grief and dismay, another reaction must surely have set in as, with swiftly mounting anger, the members of the hunting party heard the King's man give his detailed account, with its mention of Tircl's stag and Tirel's arrow and its halting conclusion of 'mischance'. An accident?—it sounded more like criminal carelessness. Walter Tirel coming into the midst of them must at once have been made aware of their suspicion, have seen their faces harden as he in turn listened horrified to the story, repeated no doubt by the eye witness with all the anxiety of one determined to exculpate himself; listened and was forced to admit its partial truth. Yes, there had been a

stag on his side and, yes, it had run 'between him and the King.'
Yes, he had 'shot at it and missed'. So many admissions that
served to augment suspicion in the minds of his hearers, the
more so given the final and seemingly damning fact: here lay
the King, an arrow through his heart, an arrow that just as the
'other archers' said had patently come from the general direction
of his, Tirel's, stand. 'Mischance'?—maybe, but regicide was a
heinous and awful thing for which the one responsible would
have to answer with his life. To Walter Tirel, as to any innocent
man accused of a crime upon evidence which he cannot at once
refute, despair must have come at that very instant when he saw,
from the hostile glances of those who mourned the King sin-
cerely, that he was not going to be believed.

In this most perilous predicament he can only have turned to
the one man present in duty bound to give him help and protec-
tion: his brother-in-law, Earl Gilbert of Tunbridge. To him
Walter must then have made for the first time the statement he
was so solemnly to reiterate over the next thirty years: 'I did not
kill the King. I was in a different part of the wood. I did not
see him at all during the hunt.' And at this point conjecture
suggests two further reasons for believing that, innocent of the
shooting, he was also entirely ignorant of the conspiracy.

First, it was not necessary for him to know anything of what
was afoot while playing his part, his innocent part, during the
hunt. And if it was unnecessary to tell him he had best not be
told; in so dark and dangerous a plot the fewer the better.
Indeed, from the little that is known about him, it may be
thought that had he been told he might have refused to take
part, might perhaps even have warned the King.

Second, to bolster the essential story of 'mischance' so as to
eliminate any possible suspicion of murder, Tirel's whole attitude
on approaching the King's body and hearing himself accused
of the shooting had to be one of utter and genuine consternation.
He must not be asked—he might not be willing—to act a part,
to express feigned horror or recite a set speech lest some unexpected question, some angry threat against him, should throw

him off balance, cause him to fluff his lines and give the game away. His dismay must be so sincere as to be immediately convincing to all present; and the surest way to achieve this would be to keep him in ignorance so that, to the charge of accidental shooting, he should have no ready answer.

But Gilbert Clare, though ready to frame his brother-in-law for the accident, had no intention that he should stand trial for regicide. Apart from any charitable thoughts for his welfare, it was in fact vital for the success of the plot that Walter should not be detained a moment longer than necessary. Were he to be allowed to argue the case in detail, to repeat too firmly—and with the support of his own attendant-archer—his assertion that he *could not* have killed the King, doubt might be sown in the minds of the King's loyal friends; and any serious inquiry would show up the fatal weakness of the 'accident' theory : its physical impossibility in terms of archery. The only safe way out, once the story of mischance had been firmly implanted, was to persuade Walter to make himself scarce. His immediate flight, strengthening the case against him, would leave unchallenged the eye-witness story so necessary both to reassure the Church and to disarm the suspicions of the dead King's supporters.

Pacing the relevant distances by the clock and making some allowances for human reaction, it would seem that not two minutes can have elapsed from the moment of the King's death to that when Tirel, standing amid the first of the hurriedly assembling members of the hunting party, listened appalled to the story told by the King's archer, backed by the Chief Hunter, and first became aware that he was the prime suspect. Turning aside within the next minute to appeal to his brother-in-law, he must at once have received the urgent advice, already determined, to mount and ride for the coast, take ship for France and there remain until the affair had blown over. Before any could stop him—if indeed, with the powerful Earl Gilbert to cover his departure, any thought to call him back—he was striding through the grove, up the rising ground to the south pass, towards the moorland between South Stricknage and the Stoney Cross road where his horses were held. Well before five past seven he must have been in the saddle and riding to the west.

The direction taken is no more than traditional, but there are good reasons for accepting the tradition as true. For one thing, Tirel himself would hardly choose to ride in the direction certain to be taken by the hunting party from which he had just been counselled to escape. He would not, therefore, take the Winchester road, not even as far as Cadenham where it branched towards Southampton. In any event, he would be ill-advised to try that port; were news of the King's death and of the manner of his killing to travel with him he might be refused permission to embark by authorities loyal to Rufus. Much the same argument would seem to apply to Lymington which lay, moreover, within the Forest boundary. To the west, however, Poole held out certain advantages. The fact that it lay in exactly the opposite direction to Winchester and at roughly the same distance from the spot where the King had fallen meant that, at the best mean speed of their horses, the two parties would be drawing apart at more than twenty-five miles an hour and every step taken by Tirel would increase both his own chances of safety and the conspirators' chances of getting rid of him without fuss. Poole was a long-established port with a considerable volume of cross-Channel trade; a ship with a crew willing to undertake the voyage would probably be easy to find. Possibly Gilbert Clare had already made sure that a ship would be waiting, to guard against a failure of the plot when the conspirators themselves might be compelled to run for their lives. At all events it seems reasonable to accept the tradition that Poole was Tirel's objective.

If so, then two things follow. He cannot have ridden alone, and he can scarcely have reached Poole that evening. Doubtless he was accompanied by his own attendant, but he would need more than that. To see him clear of the Forest and over the Avon, then set him on the right track for Poole, a guide would be wanted; and not just a forester from the limited area of the Malwood Walk, but a man of much wider knowledge of the country. It also seems possible that some sort of escort was provided, perhaps a couple of Earl Gilbert's men, as much to make sure that Walter did not change his mind as to protect him from any possible interference. At a guess, then, a party of four or five men in all.

As to the time required for the journey, there may have been some slight miscalculation owing, perhaps, to the hunt having begun rather later than expected. The straight-line distance from Stoney Cross to Poole is little more than twenty miles, but by the only sound road then available, through Ringwood and Wimborne, it would be near thirty. At the best speed possible it might take two and a half hours to cover the course, yet from the time at which Tirel rode out not more than an hour and a half of diminishing daylight remained and this, apparently, determined the guide to take the short cut from south of Ocknell Wood, over the moorland, past Burley, and so to the Avon half a mile north of Sopley. Tradition may be right in placing a smithy at what was later to be called Avon Tyrrell and in saying that there was some altercation and delay at this point; but tradition has surely strayed when it alleges that Tirel insisted on having his horse shod 'backward' to mislead the pursuit. For one thing, there were no pursuers; for another, by the time the river had been forded—quite possibly at the place now known at Tyrrell's Ford—dusk would be growing when no tracks would be discernible at all.

Upon the far bank a decision had to be taken. Ahead lay some ten miles of wild and trackless country, part wood, part marsh, with the Stour still to be forded; night would have fallen long before Poole could be reached. Rather than face these dangers it seems probable that Tirel turned south and, keeping the meandering Avon on his left hand, made for Christchurch, there to seek sanctuary for the night in Flambard's new-built priory. Setting out again at first light he may have reached Poole by sunrise, which would allow a good sixteen hours of daylight for the seventy-mile crossing to the Cotentin coast; with a fair breeze and strong oarsmen it could be done. But whether in fact he sailed from

Poole as tradition has it, or as some say from Lymington, since no incident is anywhere recorded he seems to have got back to Ponthieu without trouble or delay.

Thereafter he disappears from the story. Forty-four years were to pass before his solemn protestations of innocence were published by Suger, and by that time he and all the principal members of the hunting party were dead. But whereas the protestations had been made before witnesses who were ecclesiastics, they do not appear to have been made in secret. Some word of them must surely have reached the monkish chroniclers in England, who recorded events and sometimes gossip learned from their brethren in France; yet none mentioned the denials or thought to exonerate the Lord of Poix in his lifetime, nor was any Clare voice raised to absolve him from blame. Whilst any lived who knew the truth, the tale of Tirel's arrow and Tirel's 'mischance' must stand unquestioned.

XIV

RACE AGAINST NIGHTFALL

THE digression made necessary by the problem of Walter Tirel's flight must not be allowed to obscure the central narrative, still less to slow its pace. For now the speed of events is such that not hours but minutes become of paramount importance.

Taking into consideration the salient points of the day's happenings mentioned by the chroniclers and amplifying them with calculations based upon topography and the requirements of the hunt, the time of the King's death has been put at about five minutes to seven; it cannot, in all these circumstances, have occurred much earlier. (As a minor point, I had observed that had the hunt begun an hour, or even half an hour, earlier the King would probably not have needed to 'shield his eyes' since, with the sun to his left and still relatively high in the sky—and William of Malmesbury is positive that it was setting—he would have been standing, beneath and slightly behind his chosen tree, well within the shade of overhanging branches.) On the other hand it is certain that the hunt cannot have started any later, because of two facts that fix the estimated time of the King's death and of the hunting party's departure from the hollow with almost mathematical precision.

These facts are: 1. The hunting party, said to have left 'at once', is known to have reached Winchester that same evening. 2. Sunset that day was between 7.30 and 7.35 local apparent time (allowance made for the change in calendar). Dusk would therefore be gathering half an hour later and, even allowing for the protracted twilight of a fine summer's evening, black night would have fallen by 8.30, or, say, 8.40 at the latest. Riding after nightfall was virtually impossible, what with dangerous pitfalls

and the twofold difficulty of keeping the party together and of
finding a track, unmarked by banks or hedges. The conspirators,
moreover, would be anxious to reach the town and its castle
before the extinction of lights and the closing of gates for the
night; delays and unusual commotion were things to be avoided.
It has already been noted that the minimum riding-time for the
journey to Winchester was one and a half hours. Although this
might conceivably be reduced a little by exceptionally hard riding on a critical occasion, it would probably tend to be lengthened
again by the increasingly poor light during the latter part of the
journey. The start from the hollow must therefore have been
made not later than five minutes after seven, the King's death
having occurred less than ten minutes earlier. (In passing it
will be seen how these close measurements of time and distance,
in relation to Winchester, help to verify one of the pointers to
the site of the Rufus Stone.)

To allow for possible errors it will be well to re-examine the
time-problem, working backwards and forwards to mark the two
points that are fixed with certainty. At one end the latest time
of departure from the hollow, given the distance to be covered
and the hour of sunset; at the other the latest time of arrival at
Winchester, given the hour of nightfall. From the interval between
these two points it is next to impossible to *subtract* anything; but
if, to be on the safe side, something is *added*, if for instance the
King's death is arbitrarily made to occur nearer half-past six than
five to seven, the extra twenty minutes or so makes no important
difference to the subsequent happenings. It allows for a rather
easier ride, for a slightly earlier arrival at Winchester, in the dusk
rather than at nightfall; it cannot affect the outcome. And so
swift is the succession of events that there is neither time nor space
for the conjecture of what may have been to deviate far from
the truth of what must have been.

The present account is, of course, a long way from being the
first to grasp the significance of the hunting party's speedy action.
Other historians have noted it long ago and the sense of speed
can be detected in the accounts of the ancient chroniclers, in the

swift-moving Anglo-Saxon record as in that of Orderic Vitalis who, after describing the death of the King, goes on without pause to say that Henry 'immediately hurried to Winchester Castle where the royal treasure was kept.' What may perhaps be claimed here is that by concentrating upon the factors of time and distance something has been added not only to an understanding of the crime and its setting, but also to the appearance of premeditation. Something that amounts, or very nearly, to conclusive proof of the existence of a well-laid plan of action to follow hard upon the assassination.

Had the death really appeared to be a genuine accident to every man present, so shattering and unexpected a blow might well have provoked the sort of prolonged consternation depicted by Gaimar, in which much time would have been lost in vain lamentations followed perhaps by a more serious examination of the why and wherefore. Much of what Gaimar imagined in his poetry could have ensued, and in the end the King's body would surely have been accompanied back through the woods to the *castel*, slowly and with dignity. All this would have taken up at least an hour, possibly much more. It cannot therefore be accepted that, from the time of assembly about the body to the time of departure from the hollow, little more than five minutes elapsed —unless the plan of action was concerted beforehand.

For the time to have been cut so short all the clamour, the grief, the furious protests, the anxious questioning, must have been stilled abruptly, after an estimated two to three minutes of initial confusion, by a peremptory shout for the horses. A sharp calling to order must have followed, coupled to the announcement—made, one may guess, by Earl Gilbert on Henry's behalf—of the necessity for returning to Winchester forthwith. And this without any need for explanation just then, other than that the kingdom was in danger and nightfall only ninety minutes away.

Yet, despite the overriding need for haste, it still seems impossible to believe that the King's body was left, as so many have repeated, entirely neglected and abandoned in the woods. Because if for the shocked and sorrowing Robert fitz-Hamon such unfeeling conduct appears wholly unnatural, for Henry it seems wholly unwise. Guilty or innocent of his brother's death, to have displayed his true feelings at this moment by an act of contemptuous disrespect would have aroused the resentment if not the suspicions of the dead King's friends. To alienate the sympathies of those, outside the conspiracy, whose support might presently be invaluable would be both thoughtless and stupid, and Henry was neither.

It is therefore clear that, before the hasty departure, orders were given—by Henry himself, by Earl Gilbert, or as Gaimar seems to suggest, by Gilbert of Laigle—for the foresters under the keeper of the Walk to guard the body and in due course see that it was conveyed to the *castel*. When, some minutes later, the seven remaining members of the hunting party rode past the entrance to the *castel* inclosure—that there was no time for a halt is suggested below—a messenger must have turned aside to carry orders to either the Marshal or the Constable of the hunting-court to have the body brought to Winchester. Of this the clearest proof is that it happened, that the body was brought to the city where it arrived early on the following morning.

By the same messenger it seems probable that orders were also sent to the officials in charge to bring back to Winchester the whole of the numerous hunting-court, although neither the court nor the King's body could be brought to their destination that night. Even after the servants and menials had seen to the packing and loading of furniture and baggage, it was the pace of the pack-horses that would determine the duration of the journey. At a walk of, at best, eight miles an hour the convoy, with necessary halts, would require a good three hours to complete the distance; less than half of it could be covered before nightfall. Since the same low speed would apply to the transport of the dead King whose body had not yet been brought back from the hollow, neither party is likely to have left the vicinity of the *castel* that evening. (Little advantage would be gained by trying to reach Romsey. Although it already possessed a fine church and a famous nunnery, the village was too insignificant to afford either food or shelter to so many men and horses.)

The story goes—William of Malmesbury tells it—that the body was found lying in the woods by a charcoal-burner who covered it with a tattered cloak and carried it, apparently without authority, to Winchester upon his cart. To this a strong local tradition adds that the man's name was Purkiss and that those of the same name still living in the Forest are his lineal descendants. There are no reasons for doubting this carefully handed-down tradition any more than that concerning the site of the Rufus Stone; and it is safe to presume that the chronicler was, as usual, faithfully reporting what he had been told. Yet something about the wording of the story seems to hint—from the supposedly chance finding of the deserted body to the use of so humble a vehicle to carry it away—at the changed attitude towards the now suddenly despised Rufus. It is, perhaps, the cautious beginning of the campaign of disparagement.

How Purkiss came to be involved seems more likely to have happened in this way. During any visit to the *castel* by the King and his court a constant supply of fuel would be required for cooking and heating; since the best and safest fuel was charcoal, the charcoal-burner and his cart must have been a familiar sight in the inclosure. If in fact it was a wheeled cart and not a sled, then, in the Forest of those days, it may well have been the only one for miles around. That evening the staff of the hunting-court, hurriedly preparing to leave either that same night or early on the following morning, must have needed all the transport they could lay hands on; on a short visit with a relatively small amount of baggage and furniture, they may even have depended entirely on pack-horses and had no carts at all. Yet a cart had to be found; the King's body could not simply be slung over a horse's back like the carcass of a stag. Perhaps, then, it was not Purkiss who found the body, but the foresters who, knowing his whereabouts, found Purkiss; and that it was either the keeper of the Walk or the Constable at the *castel* who commandeered the cart and gave him his marching orders.

What is certain is that, before any serious claim to the throne could be advanced, the corpse had to be produced in Winchester. It had to be shown to the people so that all might recognize it, know that the King was dead and accept without murmur the proclaiming of a successor. It had to be seen by the clergy so that the cause of death should be established and the story of 'mischance' credited, so that, whatever earlier leakage might perhaps have caused the mysterious warnings, no ecclesiastical voice could henceforth be raised to allege foul play. So crafty a man as Henry cannot have been unaware of this twofold necessity, and it therefore seems doubly impossible to believe that he was so careless as to ride away without first giving orders for the body's disposal.

One further detail in the chronicler's account deserves a brief mention, if only because it is so often quoted with superstitious relish. It is said that, all along the road to Winchester, the King's body 'dripped blood'. Modern writers have rejected this grisly legend as a physical impossibility. And so it is; save upon the supposition that the King, though unconscious and bleeding to death, was still alive. Even so, it is hard to see how this surmise can add anything of value to the story as a whole, though it may perhaps be made to stress the speed of Henry's departure by suggesting that he did not wait to see if his mortally wounded brother was really dead.

It was neither panic nor callous neglect that governed the speed of departure, but time. And it is because so little of it was available for the ride to Winchester that it does not seem possible to allow for any halt at the *castel* itself, tempting though it is to imagine a brief visit, if only for the purpose of searching and impounding the dead King's belongings. This might perhaps have been done had the shooting taken place half an hour earlier, which all things considered does not seem likely. What does seem likely is that the seven men with their personal attendants, and that small armed escort which, it has been suggested, had in all probability accompanied the King on the way to the hunt, rode straight off from the hollow the moment the grooms had brought forward the horses from the various points near the road where they had been held since before the hunt began. The time-factor then makes it certain that between five and ten past seven at the latest the party, of perhaps twenty men in all, was riding out through the furze and the bracken and away down the ancient road towards Cadenham and Romsey.

A fine evening, in the glades and between the trees the shadows were long. High above, the sunlight that had dazzled the King still flickered through the branches and gilded the topmost leaves whilst, unnoticed, the beauty of the woodland Forest slipped past, giving way to the moor beyond Ower and the marsh by Netley as the jangling cavalcade pounded on at a hard trot. An uncomfortable ride it must have been, most of all to those in the conspiracy. To the physical discomfort of heavy jogging in an ill-shaped saddle over rough roads there was added the inescapable mental anguish; dark thoughts of the irrevocable deed that lay so close behind, stark awareness of what lay so near ahead, of the bold action yet to be taken; action that were it not taken that night might fail of its purpose and, with its failure, endanger the success of the plot and place the very lives of the plotters in jeopardy.

It may be reckoned that the first eleven miles or so—that is, eight to the crossing of the Test at Romsey, the breasting of the rise beyond, and on through the woods towards Ampfield—were covered in three-quarters of an hour, which is fast going, and that then a short halt was called. But it cannot have been more than a few minutes' breathing-space for man and beast, because the sun had now set, the shadows were deepening and not much more than forty minutes of useful light remained with nine miles still to be covered. Thereafter the hard trot must have been kept up without cease, along the woodland road winding but level past the hamlet of Hursley, until the first long ascent brought the pace down to a walk. Another level stretch over which time was made up, a sharp descent into the cool valley, and the riders were urging their tiring mounts up the steep climb to the warmer air upon the open downs.

There was no moon that night to prolong the dusk; so that it must have been by the very last glimmer of twilight that they reached the summit and, thrusting on through the treacherous shadows, at length looked down upon the darkened city, with its Saxon halls and houses huddled upon the Itchen, its great white church floating in the marsh and, close by on rising ground, the stout Norman walls of its dominant castle-palace. The race against the night had been won by a small margin. Now for the bold action.

XV

WINCHESTER

BY quarter to nine at the latest the leading members of the cavalcade must have drawn up before the castle gates, to shout an imperious demand for admittance 'in the King's name'. A pause whilst the guards within, roused to sudden activity, challenged and, receiving some sign of recognition, hurriedly unbarred and drew back the gates. Urged on again the weary horses, their hoof-beats echoing beneath the arched guard-tower, clattered into the courtyard. The riders dismounted, stiff from the twenty-mile journey; the leaders escorted by their armed attendants, stamping heavily up the steps, strode on into the central hall where servants scurried, obedient to command, bringing lights and summoning their lords to greet the high-ranking bearers of important tidings.

Since the castle of those days was also the royal palace all the members of the court—less the hunting-court still at Malwood—were probably assembled within its walls, including William Giffard, the dead King's chancellor and Gilbert Clare's uncle, and the two sons of Roger de Beaumont, Earl of Warwick: Robert, Count of Meulan, and Henry his younger brother. It may well be that all were privy to the conspiracy, or had at least had some word of it dropped to them, for there is nothing in the chroniclers' records to show that they expressed either surprise or grief at the news; and the speed with which they rallied to Henry is remarkable.

With these, with the two Clare brothers, with, apparently, Laigle and Monfichet—and there may well have been others—Henry now commanded sufficient support to see the plan through its initial and most difficult stage. Nothing seems to be known

of Robert fitz-Hamon's attitude at this time; perhaps his feelings
for the dead King were respected and he was not called upon to
express an opinion that night.[1] At all events there is no record of
any open resistance, and without delay Henry took the next
decisive step : summoned William of Breteuil before the assembly
and demanded the keys of the Treasury.

Whether what followed was an unrehearsed episode or a put-
up job to enable Henry to expound, at the earliest moment and
before the senior clerical witness, William Giffard, his legalistic
claim to the throne is hard to tell. Henry's argument smacks
strongly of lengthy premeditation, whilst the Treasurer's opposition gives an impression of genuine surprise. 'Surrender the
Treasury?' Breteuil appears to have said. 'Impossible!' He held
it on trust from the King now dead; he could give it up only to
the legitimate successor, to the heir by treaty as by primogeniture,
Robert, Duke of Normandy. To this Henry's answer—which
cannot possibly have been thought up on the spur of the moment
—was that he did not claim the treasure, or the throne, by primogeniture, but by porphyrogeniture. He had been 'born in the
purple', born after his father had been crowned King at Westminster. Seen in this light Robert, born in Normandy before the
conquest, was ruled out of the succession and he, Henry, became
the sole rightful heir.

About this theory there was nothing startlingly new, save
Henry's production of it at this moment. It had been recognized
in the Byzantine empire, where the title *'porphyrogenitus'* had
been given to Constantine VII who had died in 959. It was the
corollary that was startling : the inference that not Robert alone
but also Rufus, born before the conquest, was and always should
have been excluded from the succession since he was no more
than the son of a duke whilst Henry, born in England in 1067,
was the son of a king. It was certainly a convenient piece of
sophistry; if it was rather too soon to publish it to the laity, most

---

[1] Some have suggested that he vanished mysteriously immediately afterwards. But, although he took no further part in the proceedings, he did not
oppose Henry and survived unmolested.

of the clergy would appreciate its point at once because of a not too far-distant precedent in English history. More than that, to any who came to suspect Henry's complicity in the death of the King, and whose consciences might stir uneasily at the thought, it offered a comforting measure of justification by establishing 'the rule of porphyrogeniture' which, as Christopher Brooke puts it, 'made the murder of Rufus not an act of treachery but the removal of a blaspheming usurper.'

The English precedent was not perhaps a very happy one. It related to an earlier case of sudden death; to the murder at Corfe Castle, in 978, of the young King Edward, subsequently known as Edward the Martyr, by the supporters of the still younger prince Ethelred—later to be immortalized by Saxon wit as *Edelraed Unraed*—who, unlike his brother, had been born after their father had become king. At the time, as Eadmer was to note disapprovingly in his *Life of St Dunstan*, the 'born in the purple' theory was advanced in an attempt to prove that Ethelred was the rightful king and so, in some degree, to justify the liquidation of Edward. One hundred and twenty-two years later, when the heat had gone out of the matter, there were some who accepted without question the superior claim to the throne of one who was *porphyrogenitus*, and Henry appears to have been among them. He might have caused his brother to be murdered, no less; he seems to have brought himself seriously to believe in his right to do so.

Whether the embarrassed Treasurer was convinced by the argument or whether, just as probably, he was overawed by the powerful support arrayed on Henry's side he seems to have given in without any great show of resistance. The keys of the Treasury were presently handed over, and the first obstacle to the seizure of power had been surmounted. It seems more than likely that then, rather than wait for morning, Henry at once went to the storehouse in the keep to inspect what he had gained; not just to gloat over the gold and silver bullion glinting in the light of spluttering torches, nor to turn the leaves of the *Liber de Thesauro*, the Domesday record of all the assets now within his grasp;

but rather to gather up and set aside those things he would need to take with him upon the following morning: the jewelled gloves, the gold-threaded dalmatic mantle, the sceptre, and the crown.

Afterwards he may have sat up with William Giffard and his clerks, drafting by the light of smoking oil-wicks and horn-windowed lanterns urgent letters to those in the country upon whose support he might hope to count. One letter in particular is likely to have been prepared that night, for it was certainly completed and dispatched early next day. A letter to Anselm, then living in Lyons in self-imposed exile from Rome, giving him news of the death of Rufus and inviting him to return forthwith to his archbishopric of Canterbury. It was the first, well-advised bid to gain the favour of the Church.

At Malwood, by the first light of Friday, August 3rd, when the menials of the hunting-court were beginning to stir, to light fires and draw water, Purkiss the charcoal-burner made ready for the journey to Winchester.

It is possible, of course, that he had set out on the previous evening; but, if so, then he would not have got much beyond Romsey before nightfall and, after spending the night in the woods, would have reached the city some two hours earlier than seems probable from the chroniclers' accounts. It is therefore more likely either that he spent the night in the hollow or that he brought his cart with the dead king upon it to the inclosure at the *castel,* where the members of the court no doubt came to gape at the body. They may have done more than gape, for the 'new knight's cloak' that, according to Gaimar, had covered the body on Thursday became next morning 'a poor ragged cloak' according to William of Malmesbury. Perhaps among the court officials there were rascals like those who, at Rouen thirteen years earlier, had hardly waited for the Conqueror to breath his last before stripping the body of its clothing. It is not inconceivable that the body of Rufus was similarly robbed.

From the timing of subsequent events it seems probable that

Purkiss left the vicinity of the *castel* shortly after daybreak at half-past three and that, allowing for a cart's mean speed of little more than six miles an hour, he reached Winchester at half-past six. By that time the news of the King's death, released by the castle, must have been spreading through the town because, even as the cart with its sorry burden entered the gates to wend its way through narrow streets, the grieving crowds gathered and, Orderic Vitalis says, 'many poor people came out to follow the bier' on its way to the cathedral. When, at about seven, the cart drew up at the church door the body was received by the clergy by whom it was, presumably, officially identified since in due course 'many great men', nobles and ecclesiastics, assembled for the funeral, although, says William of Malmesbury, 'few came to mourn'— an expression of opinion which, however true, contains more than a hint of disparagement.

The hour of the funeral can be fixed within narrow limits by working backward from events known to have occurred before the ending of the day. The writer of the *Anglo-Saxon Chronicle*, after his terse summary of the death of Rufus, says: 'He was slain on the Thursday and buried next morning. After he was buried, those councillors who were close at hand elected his brother Henry to be king. He straightway gave the bishopric of Winchester to William Giffard, and then went to London.' But that compact statement conceals a wealth of detailed activity, including the final preparation of all-important letters, the packing and loading of baggage—with the precious regalia requiring special care—and the warning for duty of a sufficient number of mounted men-at-arms for a journey that was to be, even more than usual, a military operation.

Henry and his party planned to spend Friday night in the palace at Westminster. To make sure of arriving before nightfall, eight-thirty, they would allow the better part of an hour for possible delays and accidents and thus, to be on the safe side, set their proposed time of arrival at sunset, seven-thirty. The distance from Winchester to Westminster, by whatever route was chosen and wherever the Thames was crossed or forded, cannot then have been much less than seventy-two miles, whilst the pace cannot have exceeded the average of eight miles an hour, given the presence in the convoy of pack-horses and perhaps of carts. This gives the time on the road as nine hours, to which must be added an allowance for essential halts at whose number and duration one can only guess. No doubt, to speed the march, led horses were taken as remounts, and other fresh mounts might certainly be commandeered from manors and villages passed on the way; but the total time spent at halts for the refreshment of man and beast cannot have been less than two hours. The overall time required can therefore be estimated at a good eleven hours, and the start from the castle must have been made at around half-past eight in the morning.

Working back from that hour, the conference mentioned by the Anglo-Saxon chronicler at which Henry was 'elected' king and William Giffard made Bishop of Winchester, although it may have been little more than a formality, can scarcely have taken less than half an hour—bringing the time back to eight o'clock. To return to the castle from the cathedral after the funeral would take perhaps as much as a quarter of an hour, which brings the ending of the ceremony to about seven forty-five. Since Rufus was given a decent, if unspectacular burial in the presence of the 'many great men', the function must have lasted in all nearly half an hour however short it was cut, bringing the time of its starting to about quarter-past seven. Allowing for delays necessary at the cathedral and for the assembling of the notables from the castle, it can be said that Purkiss and his cart reached the church door at about seven o'clock.

The purpose of so careful an examination of the time-table of events on Friday, August 3rd, and in particular of the almost exact fixing of the hour at which the King's body reached the cathedral, is to confirm the existence of the premeditated plan of action. For without such a plan it would have been next to impossible for Henry to get through all the business done at the castle in the time available that morning. Even supposing that he and his collaborators were roused at dawn—which, given the events of Thursday evening, would permit no more than four to five hours' rest—they can hardly have been ready for work much before sun-up at four-thirty. To the time when the charcoal-burner's cart reached the cathedral this gave only two and a half hours for all the tasks requiring immediate attention; time enough for action, none for indecision.

What was done in that brief period was remarkable enough. Orders for the journey to Westminster would have been issued overnight; even so the mustering of the escort together with its mounts and remounts could not be achieved at a moment's notice. Nor could those letters to Anselm and other prelates be completed in a matter of minutes; they may have been drafted late on Thursday evening but it would be daylight before they could be written in full, and the clerks would then have to submit them to Henry for approval—read them out since he was illiterate, witness his cross and appose his seal. Such weighty correspondence would have demanded a whole morning's work had its form not been decided before the death of Rufus. Some time, moreover, must have been spent in the Treasury by Henry in person, not only to supervise the removal of the regalia, but also to collect a fair number of bags of silver and gold coin. Not as a beggar would he approach Westminster, but as king-elect, with wealth and armed force.

That most of these lengthy preparations were completed by seven o'clock seems evident, because afterwards there was no time. Even at the cathedral time must have been short. Although the clergy may have received early warning of the King's death, they had still to receive the body and make ready for a dignified funeral, however brief, setting the gravediggers to work opening the tomb beneath the central tower, giving the joiners time to prepare the coffin, meeting the 'many great men' who came, if not to mourn, at least to witness. Yet from the arrival of the body to the end of the ceremony no more than an hour can have elapsed. Like everything else that morning the interment went off with all the smoothness of a well-planned operation.

There is a crispness in the chroniclers' statement—'Rufus was buried . . . Henry was elected King . . . and went to London'— which gives to the day's events a sense, not of haste, but of fore-thought and confident action. Still more, about the whole twelve-hour period from seven o'clock on Thursday evening to seven on Friday morning when the body of Rufus was received at the church door, there is a drill-like precision that can only denote an absence of surprise at the initial event in Stricknage Wood.

XVI

WESTMINSTER

WELL before nine o'clock in the morning of August 3rd
the cavalcade, swinging away from the castle with the
new King in the midst of those 'councillors', the barons
who had recognized him, and guarded by the strong force of
mounted troops, took the road over the downs to the north-east.
The route most probably followed was that through Alton and
Farnham to Guildford, thence to Cobham and so to the Thames,
perhaps at Kingston. From the silence of the chroniclers one may
judge that no untoward incident occurred during the seventy-
mile journey and, more important, that there was no opposition.
By dusk the whole force, crossing the meadows and marshy
streams bordering the abbey lands, had come safely to the fine
new palace at Westminster built for Rufus by Flambard.

It was too late to start work that night. Tired and saddle-sore,
Henry and his companions can have wanted nothing better than
food, drink and a good night's rest. But on Saturday morning
business began early with the despatch of an envoy to request the
presence at the palace of Maurice, Bishop of London. Together
with the powerful support of the Clares, the Beaumonts and other
'councillors', Henry held the crown; what he now required was
a bishop to place it upon his head, and to do so at the crowning-
place sanctified by the Confessor and confirmed by the Conqueror.

There is nothing to show that the Bishop of London was privy
to the conspiracy against Rufus. Yet it seems possible either that
he had been sounded some time previously or that he now received
firm advice from prelates already in the know, or perhaps both,
because he appears to have acted with remarkably little reluct-

ance. At the outset he may well have counselled delay, at least
until, in the absence of Anselm, the Archbishop of York had time
to arrive. But to this the objections, doubtless raised by Henry
and his supporters, were obvious. For a messenger to reach York
and for Archbishop Thomas to get to Westminster, supposing
that he was willing to come, would take the better part of ten
days, if not more; and the danger of so long an interregnum was
patent to all, the danger of the chaos that must ensue, were the
succession to be disputed. In ten days many powerful lords, both
lay and temporal, would have time to reflect that the legitimate
heir was the elder brother, however indisputable the porphyrogeniture of the younger. Trouble in Normandy was to be expected
in any event. Robert was drawing near; within a month he would
be in his dukedom. Were there then to be no crowned head in
England, he must surely assert his legally unchallengeable treaty
rights and make a bid for the kingdom. From the strife and
anarchy that would surely follow the Church could not hope to
gain.

By such arguments Bishop Maurice may have been impressed,
but there were other cogent reasons for his submission. Henry,
in his dealings with the Church, held a strong hand from which
he had already played three good cards. First, the invitation to
Anselm; second, the appointment of William Giffard to the richest
see in England, hitherto held vacant by Rufus; third, orders given
for the arrest and imprisonment in the Tower of the late King's
chief extortioner Ranulf Flambard. He now played the ace :
produced a charter which, while it did not differ 'in essentials
from that which his predecessors had issued in similar circumstances' (Barlow), in its details gave satisfaction to the Church on
the principal heads of complaint against Rufus.

'I abolish,' said Henry, 'all the evil practices with which the
realm of England was unjustly oppressed.' The ancient law was to
be restored; vacant abbacies and bishoprics were to be filled;
recognized feudal custom would henceforth be observed. It was
an adroit piece of political chicanery that had much in common
with some modern election manifesto, in which the late King's

thirteen years of supposed misrule were roundly denounced and promises made that were unlikely to survive—and in fact did not survive—the first years of the new reign.

So comprehensive a document, vital to the granting of Henry's request for the Church's blessing, cannot have been drawn up in the course of a single forenoon. And since there had been no time for such careful work to be done between Thursday evening and early Saturday, it can only be supposed that the rough draft at least had been outlined well before the death of Rufus. Even so, after preliminary negotiations had led to general agreement, amendments of detail and re-drafting must have occupied the greater part of the morning, with the final writing, the reading out and the affixing of seals lasting into the afternoon. So that when Bishop Maurice departed, well satisfied with the completed charter, court and clergy must have set to work with a will, preparing for the next day's great occasion, rehearsing their parts for the splendid and impressive ceremony of the coronation.

Early on Sunday the Bishop returned in state, to be received at the church by the abbot. At the palace the court officials, the barons and their attendants assembled about the now gorgeously-robed figure of the new monarch, and presently moved in solemn procession to the abbey before whose door the well-armed troops stood guard, holding back the awed, staring crowd of common people. And in due course the writer of the *Anglo-Saxon Chronicle* was able to finish the narrative he had begun with the slaying of Rufus on Thursday : 'On the following Sunday, before the altar at Westminster, Henry vowed to God and to all the people to abolish all the injustices which were prevalent during his brother's reign . . . Thereafter, Maurice, Bishop of London, consecrated him King.'

It can scarcely be denied that the plan, however villainous its conception, had been brilliantly executed. On Thursday evening no more than the King's pawn, by Sunday morning the pawn was crowned; in five bold moves Henry had crossed the board. The first had seen the ride to Winchester and the seizing of the

Treasury in the name of porphyrogeniture. The second had included the recognition—the crown was never elective—by the
council of barons, the letter to Anselm and the appointment of
William Giffard. The third had brought him to Westminster, the
fourth to the production of the charter, and the fifth to the coronation with its twofold effect: the acceptance of the new King and
his many promises, the repudiation of the late King and all his
works. A decisive effect, for no one now dared to inquire, at least
not publicly, into the manner in which Rufus had come to his
sudden and, for Henry, convenient end.

Speed had been the chief ingredient of success. From the woods
to Westminster Abbey, from the hollow to the summit, a physical
distance of one hundred miles, had required only a few hours
more than two and a half days. It was not quite an all-time British
record; Harold Godwineson had done it in one. But then Edward
the Confessor had died in his bed at Westminster, and from that
bed, or so it was claimed, had named Harold as his successor.
The Witan were unanimous, Harold and the crown were in the
palace, the abbey across the way; with two invasions threatening, haste had been politically wise. Yet when, in 1087, the succession came to Rufus—who had the Conqueror's instructions
and Lanfranc's support, who was already on the Channel coast
waiting to embark when he heard of his father's death—almost
three weeks passed by before the coronation. Henry had done
better than that; given the obstacles to be overcome, he could
hardly have moved faster than he did. Only premeditation can
account for such speed.

Nor did he rest idly upon his throne after the triumphant acces-
sion. He had to make sure of continued support, guard against
the future. Many of his coronation vows were kept, for a while.
Anselm was back before Michaelmas; the vacant sees were filled,
appointments made to the abbacies whose revenues Rufus had so
long enjoyed, and among the first was that of Ely, filled by
Richard Clare, Earl Gilbert's brother. In another matter too,
Henry moved with notable speed: the matter of his marriage. So
swiftly indeed as to suggest that negotiations had been started

before the death of Rufus, possibly even by Rufus on his own account. For such a guess there is no evidence; yet, after all, the lady, Edith (Matilda), was sister to Edgar, King of Scots, who had borne the sword before Rufus at the re-enactment of the coronation ceremony in Westminster Hall in 1099. The two kings may then have broached a topic whose successful outcome would be to their mutual advantage.

Certainly the marriage plan offered great advantages to Henry. Edith was the daughter of Malcolm III and Margaret—Saint Margaret, sister of Edgar the Aetheling and direct descendant in the male line of Edmund Ironside, of Alfred the Great and the ancestral Cerdic. With her as queen, Henry's title would be immensely strengthened, and a son of the marriage would be so well and truly 'porphyrogenitus' from both sides of the bed that no future heir to Robert, claiming the crown by virtue of the treaty of succession, could hope to excite much sympathy for his cause. There would be no opposition to the matrimonial project, the Church would favour it and even the despised English would welcome a union with the ancient line of Saxon kings. With this in mind Henry initiated, or perhaps resumed, negotiations with the King of Scots, pressing the business forward so smartly that, despite the delays of distant journeyings, the marriage was celebated in November.

Henry's marriage rounds off the series of operations designed to ensure a smooth and effective transfer of power. At all points success had been achieved, the usurpation carried through without a hitch. Before long, with a firm hold upon internal affairs, he could prepare to face the external threat. It was certainly a grave one, perhaps graver than he had anticipated.

Time is now stretched. No longer is it a matter of hours and minutes, rather of months and of years. Yet the chain of events is still anchored to the starting-point; the death of Rufus still compels the actions of the King.

XVII

ALTON AND TINCHEBRAI

EARLY in September, Duke Robert arrived back in Normandy, to be greeted with tidings of the astounding events in England. Dismayed and angered at the news, he was also nonplussed. Rage though he might, his protests were of no avail. His claim to the throne was soundly based; the treaty, solemnly affirmed and attested, undeniably named him successor to Rufus. Against that there stood now the equally indisputable fact that Henry, at Westminster, had been consecrated and crowned; and after September 23rd, the date on which Anselm returned to Canterbury, it was plain as a pikestaff that in England the new King had the full support of the Church.

Henry was not to be persuaded by argument; only force could convince him. And force implied invasion, always a hazardous enterprise, requiring time to prepare and money to mount. Robert, however, had plenty of both; of time since it was too late in the season to undertake a cross-Channel expedition that year; of money because, with Rufus dead and the succession in dispute, there was no need to repay the mortgage on the duchy. With the considerable dowry brought by Sybil de Conversano and with many a Norman baron ready to back his claim, he might look forward with reasonable optimism to an invasion campaign the following summer.

No one in Robert's entourage at this time seems openly to have suggested that Rufus had been murdered. The ecclesiastically-sponsored account, based upon the eyewitness story, appears to have been accepted together with the lengthening tale of dreams, portents and weird antedated predictions now being disseminated in England. It may be that some in Normandy had their doubts, that word was spreading out of Ponthieu telling of the Lord of Poix's denial of his supposed part in the 'accident', and that the late King's death was coming to be seen as a good deal too convenient for Henry. If such suspicions were voiced they were not spoken loudly enough to be heard by the cautious chroniclers. No one demanded an inquiry and at no time does Robert appear to have levelled an accusation of fratricide against Henry; he was not out to avenge the death of Rufus, only to assert his own legitimate claim under the treaty of succession.

Nor did those barons in England who sided with Robert do so because they rejected Henry as a murderer. Some may have felt bound by oath and by law to stand firm upon the terms of the treaty, but it was feudal obligation that compelled the majority. For their lands in England they had perforce to acknowledge the newly anointed King, but for lands held in Normandy it was to Robert that they owed allegiance and military service. This divided loyalty, the enduring result of the Conqueror's deathbed decision to split the kingdom from the duchy, explains how it came about that one of Robert's supporters was his tenant Walter Giffard—son of Walter who had been the Conqueror's companion —who would otherwise, as brother of the new Bishop of Winchester and uncle to Gilbert Clare, probably have supported Henry. Others siding with Robert included William of Warenne, Earl of Surrey, one of the few who had remained unswervingly loyal to Rufus in 1088, and the three sons of Roger of Montgomery: Arnulf, Roger and that unsavoury character but brilliant fortress-builder, Robert of Belleme, who, under Rufus, had raised the first great castle at Gisors.

In February 1101 Robert received a new recruit in the person of Ranulf Flambard. How he had contrived to get out of the well-guarded Tower and then out of England remains, despite entertaining legends, something of a mystery. Admittedly, he knew every inch of the fortress from having recently rebuilt and extended its defences, but a suspicion of connivance is hard to resist. Later on, Henry was to take him back and make good use of his undoubted talents: did he then cunningly release him to act as double-agent in Robert's camp? In any event Flambard seems, temporarily at least, to have served Robert well.

Preparations for Robert's military expedition, continued during the spring, were completed by the end of June when a considerable force of men and ships was assembled upon the Normandy coast. Early in July the fleet set sail from Le Tréport and crossed the Channel without incident. Henry, informed of the sailing, marched his hastily gathered troops to the coast; but, misled as to the point of landing, was watching Arundel when Robert came ashore unopposed at Portsmouth. With surprise achieved, the invading army at once marched on Winchester whilst Henry belatedly fell back from the coast. Robert, learning at Winchester of his brother's movements, promptly marched east and, on July 21st, 1101, the opposing armies came face to face at Alton.

Robert's position was now one of great strength. Strategically he held the initiative. His army probably superior to Henry's in numbers was certainly, after the bloodless invasion, superior in morale. Legally he could claim to be the rightful king. He had but to give battle and win the day to gain the kingdom. It is sometimes said that he might have bypassed Henry and marched on London; but London, though growing in importance as a centre of commerce, was not the capital.[1] He had no need for such a march; Winchester lay behind him and its castle still held the greater part of the royal treasure. Yet, instead of advancing, he halted his army and agreed to a parley.

For this failure to follow through an overwhelming military advantage Robert's unstable character must to some extent be held responsible; he had none of his father's stern and single-minded determination to conquer, and in low cunning he was no match for his unscrupulous young brother. But there were valid reasons for not pressing the advantage too far. Robert had made no open declaration of any desire to depose Henry and have him-

[1] There was no fixed capital under the Norman kings. With all power vested in the sovereign, the 'capital' was wherever the king temporarily chose to be.

self crowned in his stead, and his restraint in this matter was certainly wise; for, as Flambard may have advised him, to displace Henry would have been difficult in the extreme, given the firm support of the Church for one they had so recently consecrated King. Nor would all of Robert's supporters, in England as in Normandy, have been ready to pick a serious quarrel with the Church in order to establish as ruler in the kingdom one who, in the past, had scarcely been competent to rule in his own dukedom. It may be that Robert, satisfied with the invasion's easy success, cared less to gain the throne by battle than to compel recognition of his right to it by treaty. Perhaps too, he was moved by that same family feeling as, ten years earlier, had inspired Rufus to let bygones be bygones. Now, rather than conquer and humiliate, he chose the gentler path of conciliation. His one mistake seems to have been that, like Rufus, he trusted Henry.

It must have been with a sigh of relief that Henry learned of Robert's readiness to parley. Much that would be put to risk in armed combat might be made safe in a brotherly conference whose results could always be denounced at a more convenient time. That he was aware of the weakness of his position seems evident from the speed with which he agreed to Robert's terms of peace whereby, in addition to granting certain lands in England, Henry promised to pay an annual indemnity that clearly recognized the validity of Robert's claim to the throne. The amount was put at two thousand pounds a year, a great sum for those days, but considering that Robert's army stood between Henry and the treasure at Winchester it was not excessive. (No exact equivalent can be determined, but in the depreciated currency of the late-20th century it might be worth two millions.)

The brothers appear to have met and parted in friendly fashion. Robert withdrew his forces to Normandy, returning thereafter on several occasions as much, or so it seems, to re-assert his rights as to claim the cash. Other than his brother's word, however, Robert held no real guarantee, so that when in due course Henry felt strong enough to refuse to continue the indemnity it became clear to Robert that the treaty of Alton was to be accorded no greater respect than the treaty of 1091, reaffirmed in 1096, which had promised him the throne in succession to Rufus. Worse than that, he no longer had the military strength to insist upon either.

What the treaty of Alton had gained for Henry was soon understood clearly on both sides of the Channel. Recognition of Robert's legal right to the throne, expressed by the indemnity, mattered to no one except to Robert himself; what did matter to all men was the admission of Henry's right of possession, no longer disputed and soon unassailable. With his power as king greatly strengthened he reached out for a power yet greater, to be found in the reunion of Normandy and England under his sole authority. What the Conqueror had held, and given up on his deathbed, what Rufus had so nearly regained, the new King of the English would seize by stealth, by ruse, at length by force. Tirelessly undermining Robert's authority he missed no chance to revile his misrule, though in fact it was no worse than that of neighbouring lands, of Anjou under Foulk *le réchin*, of the demesne of France under Philip I. The year 1105 marked the outbreak of war and the climax came in 1106 when Robert, with dwindling forces, deserted by his strongest supporters, vainly opposed Henry whose invading army was largely composed of English troops delighted to find, on Norman soil, an occasion to pay off old scores on the relatives of those who had routed their fathers at Hastings.

The end came swiftly. Late that summer Henry advanced to lay siege to Tinchebrai. Robert, with insufficient force, impetuously attempted to relieve it. No friendly parley was offered this time. Battle was joined and, after a sharp fight, Robert's army was routed and he himself taken prisoner. Henry was master of Normandy. It was September 29th, forty years to the day since the Conqueror's landing at Pevensey.

About Robert's capture—fighting sword in hand, surrounded and almost alone—there was nothing ignoble. By the code of chivalry of the age he could expect to be treated by his captor as an honoured guest, to be set at liberty either upon payment of a ransom, perhaps equivalent to the indemnity he had himself received under the treaty of Alton, or upon the granting to Henry of major territorial concessions. The treatment he got was both unexpected and exceptional. Henry, ousting him forthwith, seized the dukedom for himself and, carrying his now defenceless elder brother off to England, imprisoned him for life.

It is here that Christopher Brooke remarks that 'to imprison a great noble for life was rarely done; to imprison an elder brother almost never.' And he then points to the remarkable parallel of the Spanish brothers, of which Henry must surely have known since it was common knowledge and recent history: of Sancho murdered, of Garcia imprisoned for life, of Alfonso the survivor taking for himself the kingdoms of Castille, Léon and Galicia. But if Henry profited from this lesson in ruthless political chicanery, he must also have learned to be careful. Not the Church and its monkish chroniclers, not the restless barons of England and Normandy, not even the despised English would have swallowed, whole and without question, another story of convenient 'mischance'. Robert, desposed from the dukedom, might be imprisoned; he could not be put to death.

It is said that Robert was kept in 'honourable captivity', in the sense that he was not held in chains or thrust into a dungeon; but, however comfortable, it can scarcely have been a happy existence. Yet he survived the catastrophe at Tinchebrai by twenty-eight years. When he died, in 1134, he was eighty. In better days in Normandy his wife had given him a son and heir, known as William Clito, Count of Flanders. Made a ward of Hélias de Saint-Säens, the boy was well cared for and grew to be 'a man of great charm' whom many a Norman baron came to regard, in defiance of Henry and in the absence of Robert, as the rightful duke. It must have been a relief for Henry to learn—after the death of his own son, William, in the *White Ship* disaster of 1120 —of the death of William Clito in 1128. With the ageing Robert safely incarcerated the field was clear; and when Robert died there were no valid claimants left to dispute the crown of England.

Yet Henry's last months seem to have been clouded by miserable doubts of the future, mingled with vain regrets for the past.

Though he had recognized, and even cherished, many of his bastards he had no legitimate son to name as his successor. His daughter, the widowed Empress Matilda remarried to Geoffrey, Count of Anjou, had shown nothing but ingratitude for the favours he had conferred upon her and had at length, with the husband she despised, fomented open rebellion in Normandy. In England sycophantic clerks had flattered him with the title of 'Lion of Justice', but although he had displayed much of the stealthy ferocity of the lion his justice had been conspicuous chiefly for its cruelty. His long reign had begun like a sudden flame in the night; soon only the chilling embers remained to smoulder uncertainly. When, towards the close of 1135, his turn came to lie helpless and dying upon a bed in Normandy, he named as his heir, not his own daughter, but his favourite nephew, Stephen of Boulogne, son of the Conqueror's daughter Adela, who, for all his qualities, was to end the line of Norman kings in strife, confusion and darkness.

XVIII

INDICTMENT AND VERDICT

SUFFICIENT evidence has now been gathered concerning the death of William Rufus for certain conclusions to be reached. To begin with, in the light of the meticulous examination made of every revelant circumstance to do with either the site of the death or the conditions governing the hunt and the use of the bow, the suggestion of an accidental killing must be rejected. Revealing murder as the only alternative, the inquiry has yielded four principal suspects. The first, unavoidably, is Walter Tirel, who might be thought to have done by design what he could not have done by accident. The second is Gilbert Clare, Earl of Tunbridge, whose record and whose actions seem to prove his complicity in the crime (with the possible connivance of his uncle Walter Giffard). The third, the logically necessary assassin since 'accident' is ruled out, is the knight-huntsman, named by Gerald of Wales as 'Ranulf de Aquis', whose most probable designation was Chief Hunter in the hunting-court.

Above these three there has loomed from the start the name of the fourth : the King's younger brother Henry. From long before the shooting in Stricknage Wood, and for long years after it, his name recurs on every page of the story and is to be seen on every facet of the problem. He cannot be excluded. Not even the most partial account, biased in his favour, can lift the dark cloud of suspicion. But suspicion alone is not enough to condemn him. He must be faced, as the others have been faced, with the testing questions of motive, opportunity, and character. If he fails the test, he may be charged with murder.

It seems only wise, however, as well as fair to Henry, to cast around for other suspects; to see if any have been omitted who

should stand trial with him or even, possibly, take his place. The
difficulty here is that, in the absence of reliable documentary
evidence, one can only fall back upon legends. Not that all the old
legends, as distinct from superstitions, are devoid of interest or
even of some possible foundation in fact. There is one, for instance, involving the wife of William of Warenne, Earl of Surrey.
She, it seems, had a ward named Isabelle de Beaulieu, still a
minor in 1100, whose wardship had been claimed for the King
by feudal custom, together with the property. There was thus, it
is alleged, a strong motive, if not for killing Rufus, at least for
supporting Henry who, in his coronation charter, was to promise
that in future the relatives and not the king were to have the
wardship of a minor.

This sounds fairly plausible, until one remembers two hard
facts; the first that William of Warenne was unwavering in his
loyalty to Rufus throughout his reign, the second that, after the
murder, he supported not Henry but Robert. Nor is there any
evidence connecting the Warennes directly with the crime. Neither
William nor his wife seems to have possessed the character of an
assassin, and neither appears to have been anywhere near the New
Forest when the deed was done. Whatever half-truths may have
started it, the tale, like so many others, leads not so much up a
blind alley as into an empty room. A pity, for 'Isabelle de Beaulieu' has a romantic ring.

The sound of it led me to follow for a time the counsel of
Monsieur de Sartine; for the suggestion, contained in the legend
that some female influence had fostered the conspiracy, was certainly attractive. But for once *'cherchez la femme'* yielded little
of value. Apart from the improbable 'Isabelle', only three women
are even remotely connected with the death of Rufus.

The first and nearest is, of course, Alice Clare Tirel; and the
little known about her is chiefly to be gleaned from internal
evidence in the records of the two families. All that can safely be
said is that she and Walter were married, probably in Normandy,
perhaps at Brionne, in about 1080-5; that she seems to have lived
out her married life quietly at Poix; that she bore children, of

whom Hugh seems to have been the only male survivor; and that she subscribed frequently and generously to the great religious house at Bec and to the foundation of several churches in Ponthieu. She and Walter probably shared the rights in the manor of Langham (whose land, it will be remembered, they sold off piecemeal to provide money for Bec), but there is nothing to show that she ever went there. One may guess that at the time of the King's murder she was some thirty-five years old; if so, then she was born in Normandy before the conquest and it is quite possible that she never came to England at all. She may well have been at one with her brothers in their likely resentment at the King's retention of vacant abbacies and bishoprics; but there is no shred of evidence that she was involved in any way in the conspiracy. She must have known of her husband's departure for England in July 1100; it is most improbable that she knew of the use to which he was to be put as dupe and scapegoat.

Of the other two women, one is the allegedly beautiful and undoubtedly wealthy Sybil of Conversano, Robert's bride; the second is the pious and well-liked Edith-Matilda of Scotland, Henry's bride-to-be. Neither of them can be directly linked to the conspiracy. Indirectly, of course, Sybil is connected with it by the very fact of her marriage, by which Henry was given the first sharp warning of the further decline in his fortunes : the disturbing thought that soon he might no longer be heir-presumptive to the throne of England. But it is impossible to think of her as more than the innocent cause of any action taken by Henry. Nor can Robert himself be suspected of complicity; even supposing, without evidence, that Sybil egged him on, he had been away too far and too long to be capable of engineering the cunning 'accident' in the New Forest; and despite the ugly traits in his character he does not seem to have been the right man for coldblooded murder, still less for fratricide. To lack of opportunity and inadequacy of character may be added lack of motive; for the newly-wedded pair journeying happily to Normandy, whose mortgage they could easily pay off, there could be no incentive to kill

the King of the English, to the obvious advantage of his brother
Henry.

As for Edith-Matilda, her connection with the plot is still more
tenuous, her innocence even more certain. One may suppose that
her brother, the King of Scots, was glad enough to receive Henry's
offer of marriage in the autumn of the year 1100; and it has
already been noted that, from the speed with which it was
accepted and the arrangements concluded, it is possible to suspect that a tentative offer had been made before August. Conceivably, Henry, pointing to Robert's marriage, may have stressed
the political advisability of his own, of a union that might provide
an heir should Rufus die without issue; and Edgar, King of Scots,
may have given his agreement to the project prior to the 'accident'. But from that to suspecting Edgar of being privy to the
plot to kill his overlord the King of the English is too big a step
to take without evidence.

The name of only one other woman offers itself for brief
scrutiny: that of Adela, Henry's sister, married to the Count of
Blois. But although she was still living thirty-five years later, when
her son Stephen was able to seize the throne on Henry's death,
she can hardly have been anticipating that eventuality in August
1100. What is more, at the time of the King's murder, neither
she nor her husband appears to have made any move to join in
the struggle for power in England.

Thus, by dismissing from the case all likely females, and with
them an equal number of males, the net is drawn that much
tighter about Henry. And the time has now come to frame the
charge against him.

Of what is he suspected? In police-court language, more or less,
the indictment might read like this: that prior to August 1100
he conspired with others to kill the King and to seize the throne
for himself; that on August 2nd he caused or instigated, probably
through Earl Gilbert Clare of Tunbridge, some competent archer
—his identity is immaterial to the accusation—to shoot the King
to death in the New Forest; that he then seized the King's treasury

in Winchester where, falsely claiming to be the rightful heir, he allowed a limited council of barons to recognize him as King; and that he then proceeded to Westminster where, by means of a coronation charter, almost every one of whose promises he subsequently broke, he persuaded the Bishop of London to anoint and consecrate him in the place of the lawful successor to the throne, his brother Robert, whom he afterwards seized and imprisoned for life.

What is the evidence against him? In the absence of a direct accusation by any of his contemporaries, how strong is the circumstantial evidence? What is revealed by the three factors of motive, opportunity and character?

Motive. No one in England had a stronger motive for wishing to eliminate Rufus before Robert returned to Normandy. On this point modern historians are agreed. Poole notes that, of all others, Henry 'had most to gain by his brother's death'; Barlow says that, with Robert drawing near accompanied by a wife from whom he might soon expect a son, 'Henry's term as heir-presumptive was almost at an end'; to this Brooke adds that 'August 1100 might well seem his last real chance of securing the English throne'.

In fairness to Henry it may be conceded that there must have been, then as always, aggrieved individuals who would gladly encompass the death of a king. But in those days single-handed regicide was very uncommon, for one thing because it was uncommonly dangerous. This was not the age of the crackpot revolutionary, and any would-be assassin with a modicum of sense would certainly be deterred by the knowledge of what, even if he succeeded, would be done to him afterwards. The hideous, but not exceptional, punishments meted out in 1096 to the defeated rebels of the previous year would still, in 1100, be fresh in the minds of all men. No motive of personal revenge would seem strong enough to tempt the unassisted individual to take so fearful a risk. But what, motive apart, argues conclusively against the possibility of a lone, self-inspired assassin is that, had there been one, all Henry's friends and, in their wake, all the chroniclers would have been quick to publish the fact. It would have averted from Henry as from the Church all suspicion of complicity in the crime without the need to fabricate the accusation against Walter Tirel.

Conclusion : the only motive sufficient to incite the murder of the King was the prospect of gaining the crown, and only Henry could hope to gain it.

Opportunity. No one can have had better opportunities for hatching a plot than Henry. At the King's court he seems to have been free to come and go as he pleased; and whatever the King may at times have recalled of his younger brother's past actions in Normandy it is unlikely that he had any suspicion of possible treachery in England or he would hardly have included him in the informal hunting party to the New Forest.

At Easter, 1100, the King wore his crown in Winchester. A few weeks later he travelled to Westminster, where he held court at Whitsun; not long afterwards the court returned to Winchester. It seems to have been some time before Easter when the first surprising news came in of Robert's marriage in Apulia; possibly between Easter and Whitsun when it was learned that the journey back to Normandy had started. Henry and his presumed associates had then to reckon that Robert might reach the duchy by mid-August. This would give them a good two months in which to work out a plan of action.

Nothing is known of Henry's activities during this period; all that can be said is that he had both time and opportunity to determine the secret details of the plot. Time, and opportunity, to sound opinion among those bishops and barons at court who muttered against the King's abuses of feudal custom and who derived little comfort from the thought that Robert was heir to the throne—and for the heir-presumptive to discuss privately the situation that would arise were the King to die was not treasonable, many must have been pondering it for years. Time, too, to consult Gilbert Clare, and for Gilbert to approach his uncle William Giffard with the searching question whether, were an 'accident' to befall the King, he would support Henry against Robert on the grounds of porphyrogeniture. Time, once the 'accident' had been outlined, for Gilbert to summon his tenant and brother-in-law, Walter Tirel, who might so easily be blamed for an accident but whom no one could suspect of malice. Time, once the Forest was reached towards the end of July, to rope in the expert archer, the knight-huntsman named by Gerald of Wales. Time thereafter to watch, perhaps for several days; at length to make sure of every detail during that last morning when the King was so mysteriously, and so conveniently, indisposed and unable to hunt. Time to organize the evening shoot in the nearby hollow, to place the unsuspecting guest, to set the trap.

None of that is more than reasonable conjecture. What is certain is that Henry, immediately upon the King's death, seized the supreme opportunity and acted as only one long-prepared for the event could have acted.

Character. A man may have the strongest of motives and every possible opportunity and still be incapable of killing his brother. Fratricide, though not unknown to history, is at least unusual. Had Henry possessed a gentle nature, a placid temperament, had he shown himself to be consistently frank, considerate and just to all men, it might seem preposterous to suspect him of so black a deed. Revealed by the actions of his reign, his character displays none of those virtues. A competent but ruthless ruler, unscrupulous, violent and merciless, he was more than commonly lustful, insatiably avaricious, deliberately and excessively cruel. About these vices there is no doubt, yet it is in the later stages of his life that they are most clearly to be discerned. One sombre fact stands out from the earlier years. Long before his reign began Henry had already committed murder with his own hands.

The story is well known and hardly ever omitted even from minor histories. The curious thing is that it is seldom used to illustrate the character already formed ten years before the death of Rufus. It happened in Normandy in 1090, at the time when Henry was siding with Robert against Rufus in the struggle for control of the dukedom. There had been demonstrations in Rouen in favour of Rufus; Henry had helped to suppress them. Capturing one of the leaders, a prominent citizen by name Conan, he had him brought up to the castle battlements where he greeted him courteously, bidding him admire the view from between the crenellations. Then, standing behind the man as he peered out, he suddenly tipped him up by the heels and dropped him over the wall to his death upon the rocks below.

It may of course be urged that, although this unpleasant story of coldly calculated homicide proves Henry to have been a murderer, it still does not prove that he could have murdered his brother. But to Henry this was no well-liked member of a happy and united family; Rufus was the King whose wealth he coveted, whose power he envied, to whom he had not always been loyal, against whom, and against Robert, he had once fought until compelled by armed might to surrender. Above all Rufus was one who, by 'the rule of porphyrogeniture' upon whose validity Henry was to base his claim, had no right to be King at all. From acting upon that rule in order to gain the crown, no remaining sentiments of brotherly love would restrain so ruthlessly feral a character.

Thus, in each category, the facts point unerringly to one man as primarily responsible for the murder of the King. Henry, with Rufus slain and Robert still at a distance, would find it easy to seize the throne—*motive*. Henry, with his necessary accomplices, was a member of the hunting party—*opportunity*. Henry was a proven murderer—*character*. To no other man, or group of men, do all three of these basic requisites apply. The case against him appears to be overwhelming, and the only defence is doubt. But not even doubt can silence the incontrovertible evidence of events subsequent to the crime; events, connected and successive, that ring out like the steady chiming of a punctual clock whose mechanism must, by the very fact of its smooth operation, have been set in motion beforehand. Consider the time-factor again : the sudden death and the ride to Winchester, the claim to the throne and the seizure of the Treasury, the arrival at Westminster armed with the recognition of the barons—and a ready-made charter to placate the Church—all done within twenty-four hours ! Such speed in action proclaims a lengthy planning. It cannot have been improvised.

In a passage on 'The Treatment of Evidence', J. H. Round (in *Feudal England*) wrote that 'the paraphrasing of evidence is the work of a reporter; from the historian we have the right to expect the skilled summing up of the judge.' In justice to Henry let us see how the three modern historians, already quoted in these pages, sum up the evidence against him.

A. L. Poole, who is far from prejudiced against Henry, agrees that there are 'some facts which look ugly, which seem to suggest a plot'. To this he adds that 'his [Henry's] actions seem to be premeditated', and he notes that the seizing of the Treasury is commonly 'the first act of a usurping king'.

Christopher Brooke, examining the problem at greater length, says: 'It is impossible to avoid altogether the suspicion that Rufus's death was the result of a conspiracy in which his younger brother and successor was involved.' He is impressed by the time-factor: 'The speed of Henry's seizure of the throne is very striking'. Noting that Robert might be expected to reach Normandy in August and, further, the proximity of the scene of the King's death to Winchester, he asks: 'Is it not a strange coincidence that Rufus died in that month, and in that part of England?' His conclusion is that 'If Rufus's death in August 1100 was an accident, Henry I was an exceptionally lucky man.'

Frank Barlow goes further still: 'If Rufus did not die through a common hunting accident we may think Henry guilty.' His concise account of the King's death ends like this: 'he was killed by an arrow thought to have been shot by Walter Tirel . . . If it was murder . . . then William's brother, Henry, was certainly implicated.' And he is positive that 'the speed with which Henry acted after the death of his brother shows that he was prepared for such an emergency.'

The conclusion to be drawn from these opinions seems to be: that if the King was not shot by the 'accident' attributed by Henry and his supporters to Walter Tirel, the shooting must have been deliberate, and that if it was deliberate then Henry, as chief beneficiary, must have been the chief instigator of murder.

It has already been shown that, in all the circumstances, accidental shooting was impossible, and we may now re-call four witnesses who do not subscribe to the officially disseminated story. In approximately chronological order, they are :

Anglo-Saxon chronicler : 'The King was shot by one of his men'. (Tirel was not 'one of his men'.)
Geoffrey Gaimar : 'We do not know who shot the King'. (It only 'seemed' to be Tirel, 'because he fled'.)
Walter Tirel (repeatedly, and on his deathbed) : 'I did not shoot the King'.
Gerald of Wales : 'The King was shot by Ranulf de Aquis'.

Bearing these statements in mind, we may turn back to the evidence gained, first, from the careful scrutiny made of every pointer to the site, and then from the step-by-step examination of the Stricknage woods. Taking into consideration every relevant detail mentioned by various chroniclers and Forest historians, as well as every circumstance of topography, this evidence appears to prove conclusively :

1. That the Rufus Stone in fact marks the spot near which—within a few feet either way—the King stood and fell.

2. That Walter Tirel's three-point declaration—that he did not shoot the King, that he was in a different part of the wood, that he did not see the King at all during the hunt—is borne out by local conditions, by the limitations of archery and by the instinctive habits of hunted deer.

3. Therefore, that the shooting must have been done deliberately by some skilled archer suitably placed and acting upon orders which, for a crime of such magnitude, can only have been given, directly or through an accomplice, by the man who had most to gain.

From this it would seem that the verdict is inevitable. Henry is guilty. To gain the crown he murdered the King.

XIX

END OF THE QUEST

TO get a clear perspective of what I had seen and tried to describe I allowed a year to pass before returning to the Forest; and then, as luck would have it, I chose a month that came near to establishing a record for rainfall. When at length the sun shone again, briefly and from cloud-flecked skies, I went back to the hollow to find it deserted. The Stricknage woods were greener than ever and the glade was a swamp.

Save for the need to amend the sketch-map, no particular point at issue compelled my return. If one thing more than another drew me back it was the impulse that had first drawn me out: 'The study of medieval history,' says Christopher Brooke, 'is largely detective work, and there is no reason why it should not be widely enjoyed as such.' Back at the Stone, my own enjoyment was enhanced by the thought that it must in the nature of things be somewhat rare for a detective investigating an ancient crime to find its scene so little touched by time that he can trace the sequence of events more easily on the spot than on paper. And it was no small part of my renewed pleasure to know that what I had found here might perhaps add a footnote to an obscure page of English history.

It was July when I returned, and early morning. The wrong month and the wrong time of day for a true mental picture to be formed of the climax of August 2nd. Yet it did occur to me that perhaps it was during the morning when the King lay indisposed at the *castel* that the Chief Hunter, bringing with him the keeper of the Walk, came down here on the pretext of finding a suitable hunting-ground should the King choose to ride out that evening, in reality to inspect the grove and the marsh, to select stands for the King and Tirel, to pace the distances and set the trap he intended to spring if opportunity offered. Staring out at the curve of the North wood whence the deer would be driven, at the line of the South wood hiding Tirel's notch, I could almost see the Hunter point and hear him give his orders.

Such flights of fancy must be curbed lest they come to be mistaken for the truth. Here and now, rather than commune with Forest ghosts, I would sooner have talked with the Forest historians. With Cornish, whose clear understanding of local conditions brought him so near to the mystery's solution. With Wise who, with his expert knowledge, might easily have solved the problem, had his vision not been obscured by a detestation of Rufus surpassing even that felt by Freeman. A scholar inclined to arrogance, he lacked the humility to perceive how much might be gained from the simple and enduring local tradition : 'the history of the vulgar and the stumbling-block of the half-learned' was how he dismissed it. Yet he, too, came near to the truth : Tirel, he declared after careful study of the evidence available to him, 'certainly did not shoot the arrow'.

As for Freeman, drawn off by the false scent deliberately laid, by the dreams and portents, by the appearance of angelic messengers and goats and a pool bubbling blood at Finchhamsted, he hardly bothered to look for the truth when he came to the Forest. 'I have been on the spot,' he wrote with unconscious irony, but he 'saw nothing', nothing at all. Perhaps it is just as well; with his romantic vision and his misconstruing of Latin texts that so irritated Round he might have given us another piece of 'history in masquerade'. Instead, he went back to his enchanted task of 'gathering all the rumours which floated round the event', as Brooke puts it, and thus 'immensely increased the atmosphere of mystery'. In the end he seems scarcely to have known what it was he was looking for, and to have thought it best seriously to attribute the King's death to God's judgment upon an unspeakably wicked man.

Margaret Murray summed Freeman up as one 'entirely biassed by the ecclesiastical point of view' who acknowledged himself

'totally unable to understand the character of Rufus'. Not that
she herself can have understood it very well, or she would never
have made the extraordinary suggestion that this boisterously ener-
getic, successful and forward-looking King ordered Tirel, in the
name of some wholly incredible 'god of the witches', to shoot
him dead—and 'So I will, my lord,' says Tirel without turning a
hair. But where, the King's character apart, both she and Freeman seem to have gone wrong when they came to inquire into the
killing of the King is in their failure to realize from the start that
the 'accident' formed the keystone of the plot. Once it was
accepted, with Tirel in flight and beyond questioning, with the
swift amassing of portents to confirm the 'mischance' by making
it appear a plausible act of God, all need for an inquiry was immediately averted. And the lack of any inquiry, noted by all
modern historians, is so marked a feature of the mystery that,
put in simple terms, it may recall a famous passage in the Sher-
lock Holmes adventure of *Silver Blaze*.

Slightly parodied, it might read like this : 'Let me remind you,
Watson, of the incident of the inquiry held after the murder.'
'But there was no inquiry held after the murder.' 'That,' said
Holmes, 'is the incident.' Here too the 'incident' points the way.
It points to the only man who, after the death of Rufus, had both
the need to suppress the inquiry and the power to do so.

Henry's success in concealing his responsibility for the murder,
and even that it was murder at all, can be measured by the fact
that for more than eight centuries Englishmen continued to give
credence to the tale that Tirel was the author of the 'accident',
whether by chance or by design, until the patriotically anglicized
'Sir Walter Tyrrell' became almost as well-known a villain-hero
as Guy Fawkes. With the monkish chroniclers obediently con-
signing Rufus and all his works to the devil, Henry seemed for
long to be disproving the proverbial impossibility of 'fooling all
of the people all of the time'. He had committed the almost per-
fect crime. Only one precaution was omitted : he should have
cut down the tell-tale trees in the Stricknage woods.

Evidence is lacking to show where or when, during his reign, he hunted in the New Forest. But it does not seem that he ever revisited the Malwood Walk, and the 'castel' appears to have been allowed to fall into disrepair. Perhaps he thought the place was haunted. Some say it is, to this day.

My task of map-checking at an end, I took time off and let imagination play. Stood at the corner of the grove and fancied I could see a stag run and Tirel's shaft fall; see the Chief Hunter swing round with four seconds to spare, see him draw, aim and loose; hear the snap of the bowstring, the arrow's brief whisper. And upon the instant I found myself wishing I could have warned the King. Have sent a shout ringing back across the centuries, enough to make him spring aside in the last split-second of life before the arrow struck. After all, whatever his faults, he was a capable king and a better man than Henry. He was not a cruel tyrant and he was not a coldblooded murderer; Henry was both.

To cover up the murder of his brother, Henry murdered his brother's reputation. And the bishops, having accepted the claim of porphyrogeniture that reduced his brother from king to usurper, were compelled to follow suit. Thereafter, by the hands of the chroniclers, they so blackened the memory of William Rufus that to this day the very name carries to English ears a sound at once wild, savage, and darkly evil : 'the worst king' in our history. Yet, seen by the light of his actions, Rufus does not glow so balefully. 'He confirmed the royal power in England', says Frank Barlow, 'and he restored the ducal rights in Normandy, yet never made a sad labour of his humdrum task.' Placed beside Henry he appears almost benign. In an age when blinding was the common punishment for rebellion against the king or for defiance of his laws, a penalty that evoked no word of protest from the Church, Rufus put out far fewer eyes than had the Conqueror before him and fewer still than did Henry after him; nor did he torture, mutilate or put to death without cause and without trial as Henry was so frequently to do.

The more tangible achievements of his reign are still to be seen in England. There was no slowing down in his time of the riot of building begun under the Conqueror; the unfinished works were completed, the new projects tackled without cease. The castles spread, the great cathedrals rose up: Lincoln and Gloucester, Carlisle, Lindisfarne, Christchurch and Durham, and the first great Hall at Westminster. All men recall how they worked, those Normans, with what inexhaustible energy, with what bold and self-confident genius. But few remember that for thirteen years Rufus was their capable leader, tireless and ebullient, a necessary king, of sufficient strength to maintain what his father had gained and to preserve for posterity the hard-won unity of England.

What then, Freeman's unwarranted accusation of sodomy apart, is the gravamen of the case against William Rufus? That he exacted money from the Church? There, admittedly, he went openly beyond the limits set by feudal custom; and his high-handed action earned him, long before his death, the far from disinterested enmity of the Church. Henry flattered the Church and, by taking large numbers of ecclesiastics into his service, was able to extort the money with the Church's help. In the end it came to the same thing. The revenues from sees and abbacies purposely held vacant were soon flowing into Henry's coffers as steadily as they had flowed into those of his brother. Under Rufus the see of Canterbury had been without an archbishop for four years after the death of Lanfranc; under Henry there was to be no archbishop for five years after the death of Anselm.

But where Rufus grasped to spend lavishly, Henry was grasping and miserly. Where Rufus, whatever his secret urges, kept his lust within reasonable bounds, Henry's notorious lasciviousness went unchecked. And where Rufus seems to have shown at all times a rough and ready sense of humour, Henry seems never to have shown any—unless he counted as a joke the ever-lengthening list of his illegitimate children; it must have become a stale joke by the end of his reign, by which time he had openly acknowledged upwards of twenty bastards. From these, injected into a population of little more than a million and a quarter, there sprang in due course through the passing centuries and the fusion of the races a host of Englishmen and their descendants overseas who might—and did, and still do—claim Henry as their ancestor. Henry would not have been pleased could he have known; he loathed the English, where Rufus only laughed at them.

The quest was at an end. For the last time I looked round at the marshy glade and at the woods that, held by the clay and the gravel, have stood in almost changeless immobility since that sunlit evening long ago when the arrows flew and a King fell dead. Then, turning away from the Rufus Stone, I set out down the road for the inn at Canterton. I had not gone ten paces before it started to rain; soon it was pouring. And finding no change in the weather, and little enough in the affairs of men, I let the old chronicler have the last word: 'It rained all summer long and the taxes were very oppressive.' It did, and they are. 'What times we live in!'

SOURCES

MEDIEVAL HISTORIANS

Anglo-Saxon Chronicle. For the year 1100. *Trans* G. N. Garmonsway. Dent, 1960.

Eadmer. *Life of St Dunstan.* Rolls Series. London, 1884.

Geoffrey Gaimar. *Estorie des Engles.* Rolls Series. *Ed* A. Bell, Oxford, 1960.

Gerald of Wales. *De instructione principum* and *Gemma ecclesiastica.* Rolls Series. *Autobiography, comp* H. E. Butler. London, 1937.

John of Salisbury. *Vita Anselmis. Ed* J. P. Migne. Paris, 1855.

Orderic Vitalis. *Historia ecclesiastica. Trans* F. Forester, London, 1853-6, Also *ed* A. Le Prevost & L. Delisle, Paris, 1838-55.

Suger. *Vie de Louis VI le Gros. Ed* H. Waquet. Paris, 1929.

William of Malmesbury. *Gesta Regum.* Rolls Series. *Ed* W. Stubbs. 1889.

MODERN HISTORIANS

Barlow, Frank. *The Feudal Kingdom of England, 1042-1216.* London, 1955.

Brooke, Christopher. *The Saxon and Norman Kings.* Batsford, 1963.

Douglas, David C. *William the Conqueror.* Eyre & Spottiswoode, 1964.

Fisher, H. A. L. *A History of Europe.* Arnold, 1936.

Freeman, E. A. *The Reign of William Rufus.* Oxford, 1882.

Murray, Margaret. *God of the Witches.* Faber, 1951.

Norwich, J. J. *The Normans in the South (1016-1130).* Longmans, 1967.

Poole, A. L. *From Domesday Book to Magna Carta.* Oxford, 1951.

Richard, A. *Histoire des Comtes de Poitou.* Paris, 1903.

Round, J. H. *Feudal England.* London, 1895.

NEW FOREST HISTORIANS

Cornish, C. J. *The New Forest*. Seeley, 1894. Revised ed, 1910.

Edlin, H. L. *ed. Forestry Commission Guide to the New Forest.* (Including authoritative studies of history, geology, flora and fauna.) HMSO, 1961.

Vesey-Fitzgerald, Brian. *A Portrait of the New Forest*. Hale, 1966.

Wise, H. R. *The New Forest, its History and Scenery*. Gibbings, 1863, and 3rd ed, Sotheran, 1880.

AUTHORITIES CONSULTED

Archives Départementales de la Gironde, Bordeaux.

Archives Départementales de la Vienne, Poitiers.

Deputy Surveyor of the New Forest, Forestry Commission, The Queen's House, Lyndhurst, Hants.

HM Nautical Almanac Office, Royal Greenwich Observatory, Herstmonceux, Sussex.

The Royal Toxophilite Society, London.

INDEX

The name 'Rufus', within entries, refers to William Rufus, King; Henry, to Count Henry, later King Henry I; Robert, to Robert, Duke of Normandy; and Tirel, to Walter Tirel III, Lord of Poix.

If you have found this book interesting . . .

. . . there are almost certainly other David & Charles titles you would like to read.

Arthur: Roman Britain's Last Champion (35s), a new and exciting documentary study, contemporary in approach, by Beram Saklatvala who has an expert knowledge of Roman Britain and its aftermath. Arthur emerges as an immensely dominating figure, both triumphant and tragic, and of a calibre which makes comprehensible his permanent adoption as a national hero by the very people he so bitterly fought.

The Mines of Mendip by J. W. Gough (42s) A royal hunting forest in the Middle Ages, the limestone tableland of the Mendip Hills was for centuries one of the principal lead mining districts in England. The Romans were raising and smelting lead there within six years of their occupation of Britain, and the industry did not finally become extinct until well into the present century. Dr Gough's book is the definitive history of the long and chequered career of these ancient and once famous industries.

Old . . . a series of contemporary studies in local history. The books are mainly concerned with the period since 1750 and have a bias towards social and economic history with special reference to the visible remains of yesterday. **Old Cotswold** by Edith Brill, **Old Devon** by W. G. Hoskins, **Old Dorset** by M. B. Weinstock, **Old Mendip** by Robin Atthill, **Old Nottingham** by Malcolm Thomis, **Old Southampton Shores** by J. P. M. Pannell and **Old Yorkshire Dales** by Arthur Raistrick (All 40s).

The Industrial Archaeology of the British Isles. This is a 3-part series. The first group of books, edited by Dr E. R. R. Green, consists of regional history and eventually this will cover the whole of the British Isles. The second group of volumes examine smaller areas in greater detail. Finally there are volumes on specific subjects. All books have the same format, and this is also shared by David and Charles' other Industrial Histories.

Dartmoor by Helen Harris (50s), **The East Midlands** by David M. Smith (45s), **Gloucestershire Woollen Mills** by Jennifer Tann (45s), **Scotland** by John Butt (50s), **Southern England** by Kenneth Hudson (45s), **Stone Blocks and Iron Rails** by Bertram Baxter (45s), **The Tamar Valley** by Frank Booker (45s) and **Techniques of Industrial Archaeology** by J. P. M. Pannell (35s).